The wonder: a woman keeps a secret. A comedy. As it is now acted at the Theatres-Royal in Drury-Lane and Covent-Garden. Written by Mrs. Cent Livre. The sixth edition.

Susanna Centlivre

PRINT EDITIONS

Eighteenth Century
Collections Online
Print Editions

Gale ECCO Print Editions

Relive history with *Eighteenth Century Collections Online*, now available in print for the independent historian and collector. This series includes the most significant English-language and foreign-language works printed in Great Britain during the eighteenth century, and is organized in seven different subject areas including literature and language; medicine, science, and technology; and religion and philosophy. The collection also includes thousands of important works from the Americas.

The eighteenth century has been called "The Age of Enlightenment." It was a period of rapid advance in print culture and publishing, in world exploration, and in the rapid growth of science and technology – all of which had a profound impact on the political and cultural landscape. At the end of the century the American Revolution, French Revolution and Industrial Revolution, perhaps three of the most significant events in modern history, set in motion developments that eventually dominated world political, economic, and social life.

In a groundbreaking effort, Gale initiated a revolution of its own: digitization of epic proportions to preserve these invaluable works in the largest online archive of its kind. Contributions from major world libraries constitute over 175,000 original printed works. Scanned images of the actual pages, rather than transcriptions, recreate the works *as they first appeared.*

Now for the first time, these high-quality digital scans of original works are available via print-on-demand, making them readily accessible to libraries, students, independent scholars, and readers of all ages.

For our initial release we have created seven robust collections to form one the world's most comprehensive catalogs of 18th century works.

Initial Gale ECCO Print Editions collections include:

History and Geography
Rich in titles on English life and social history, this collection spans the world as it was known to eighteenth-century historians and explorers. Titles include a wealth of travel accounts and diaries, histories of nations from throughout the world, and maps and charts of a world that was still being discovered. Students of the War of American Independence will find fascinating accounts from the British side of conflict.

Social Science

Delve into what it was like to live during the eighteenth century by reading the first-hand accounts of everyday people, including city dwellers and farmers, businessmen and bankers, artisans and merchants, artists and their patrons, politicians and their constituents. Original texts make the American, French, and Industrial revolutions vividly contemporary.

Medicine, Science and Technology

Medical theory and practice of the 1700s developed rapidly, as is evidenced by the extensive collection, which includes descriptions of diseases, their conditions, and treatments. Books on science and technology, agriculture, military technology, natural philosophy, even cookbooks, are all contained here.

Literature and Language

Western literary study flows out of eighteenth-century works by Alexander Pope, Daniel Defoe, Henry Fielding, Frances Burney, Denis Diderot, Johann Gottfried Herder, Johann Wolfgang von Goethe, and others. Experience the birth of the modern novel, or compare the development of language using dictionaries and grammar discourses.

Religion and Philosophy

The Age of Enlightenment profoundly enriched religious and philosophical understanding and continues to influence present-day thinking. Works collected here include masterpieces by David Hume, Immanuel Kant, and Jean-Jacques Rousseau, as well as religious sermons and moral debates on the issues of the day, such as the slave trade. The Age of Reason saw conflict between Protestantism and Catholicism transformed into one between faith and logic -- a debate that continues in the twenty-first century.

Law and Reference

This collection reveals the history of English common law and Empire law in a vastly changing world of British expansion. Dominating the legal field is the *Commentaries of the Law of England* by Sir William Blackstone, which first appeared in 1765. Reference works such as almanacs and catalogues continue to educate us by revealing the day-to-day workings of society.

Fine Arts

The eighteenth-century fascination with Greek and Roman antiquity followed the systematic excavation of the ruins at Pompeii and Herculaneum in southern Italy; and after 1750 a neoclassical style dominated all artistic fields. The titles here trace developments in mostly English-language works on painting, sculpture, architecture, music, theater, and other disciplines. Instructional works on musical instruments, catalogs of art objects, comic operas, and more are also included.

The BiblioLife Network

This project was made possible in part by the BiblioLife Network (BLN), a project aimed at addressing some of the huge challenges facing book preservationists around the world. The BLN includes libraries, library networks, archives, subject matter experts, online communities and library service providers. We believe every book ever published should be available as a high-quality print reproduction; printed on-demand anywhere in the world. This insures the ongoing accessibility of the content and helps generate sustainable revenue for the libraries and organizations that work to preserve these important materials.

The following book is in the "public domain" and represents an authentic reproduction of the text as printed by the original publisher. While we have attempted to accurately maintain the integrity of the original work, there are sometimes problems with the original work or the micro-film from which the books were digitized. This can result in minor errors in reproduction. Possible imperfections include missing and blurred pages, poor pictures, markings and other reproduction issues beyond our control. Because this work is culturally important, we have made it available as part of our commitment to protecting, preserving, and promoting the world's literature.

GUIDE TO FOLD-OUTS MAPS and OVERSIZED IMAGES

The book you are reading was digitized from microfilm captured over the past thirty to forty years. Years after the creation of the original microfilm, the book was converted to digital files and made available in an online database.

In an online database, page images do not need to conform to the size restrictions found in a printed book. When converting these images back into a printed bound book, the page sizes are standardized in ways that maintain the detail of the original. For large images, such as fold-out maps, the original page image is split into two or more pages

Guidelines used to determine how to split the page image follows:

• Some images are split vertically; large images require vertical and horizontal splits.
• For horizontal splits, the content is split left to right.
• For vertical splits, the content is split from top to bottom.
• For both vertical and horizontal splits, the image is processed from top left to bottom right.

THE
WONDER:

A

WOMAN keeps a SECRET.

A

COMEDY.

As it is now Acted at the

THEATRES-ROYAL in DRURY-LANE
and COVENT-GARDEN.

Written by Mrs. CENTLIVRE

THE SIXTH EDITION.

LONDON

Printed for T. LOWNDES, W. BATHOE,
T. CASTON and W. NICOLL

M. DCC. LXVI

THE
WONDER:

A
WOMAN keeps a SECRET.

A
COMEDY.

As it is now Acted at the

THEATRES-ROYAL in DRURY-LANE and COVENT-GARDEN.

Written by Mrs. CENT LIVRE.

THE SIXTH EDITION.

LONDON:

Printed for T. LOWNDES, W. BATHOE, ·T. CASLON and W. NICOLL.

M. DCC LXVI.

PROLOGUE.

OUR Author *fears the Criticks of the Stage,*
   Who, like Barbarians, spare nor Sex, nor Age:
She trembles at those Censors in the Pit,
Who think Good-Nature shews a Want of Wit:
Such Malice, O! what Muse can undergo it?
To save themselves, they always damn the Poet.
Our Author flies from such a partial Jury,
As wary Lovers from the Nymphs of Drury:
To the few candid Judges for a Smile
She humbly sues to recompence her Toil.
To the bright Circle of the Fair, she next
Commits her Cause, with anxious Doubts perplext.
Where can she with such Hopes of Favour kneel,
As to those Judges, who her Frailties feel?
A few Mistakes, her Sex may well excuse,
And such a Plea, No Woman *shou'd refuse:*
If she succeeds, a Woman *gains Applause;*
What Female *but must favour such a Cause?*
Her Faults——whate'er they are—e'en pass 'em by,
And only on her Beauties fix your Eye.
In Plays, like Vessels floating on the Sea,
There's none so wise to know their Destiny.
In this, howe'er, the Pilot's Skill appears,
While by the Stars his constant Course he steers;
Rightly our Author *does her Judgment shew,*
That for her Safety she relies on You.
Your Approbation, fair One's, can't but move
Those stubborn Hearts, which first you taught to love:
The Men must all applaud this Play of Ours,
For who dare see with other Eyes than yours?

     Dramatis

Dramatis Personæ.
At DRURY-LANE, 1765.
MEN.

Don Lopez,	a Grandee of *Portugal*,	Mr. *Baddeley*.
Don Felix,	{ his Son, in Love with *Violante*, }	Mr. *Holland*.
Frederick,	A Merchant, - -	Mr *Packer*.
Don Pedro,	Father to *Violante*, - -	Mr *Burton*.
Col. Britten,	A Scotchman, - - - -	Mr *Palmer*.
Gibby,	His Footman, - - - -	Mr. *Johnston*.
Lissardo,	Servant to *Felix*, - -	Mr. *Yates*.

WOMEN.

Donna Violante,	{ Design'd for a Nun by her Father, in Love with *Felix*, }	Miss *Pope*.
Donna Isabella,	Sister to *Felix*, - - - -	Miss *Plym*.
Flora,	Her Maid, - - - - -	Mrs. *Clive*.
Ines,	Maid to *Violante*, - -	Mrs *Bradshaw*.

✠✠✠✠✠✠✠✠✠✠✠✠✠✠✠✠✠✠✠✠✠✠✠✠

Dramatis Personæ.
At COVENT-GARDEN.
MEN.

Don Lopez,	a Grandee of *Portugal*,	Mr. *Bennet*.
Don Felix,	{ his Son, in Love with *Violante*, }	Mr. *Ross*.
Frederick,	A Merchant, - - - -	Mr. *Anderson*.
Don Pedro,	Father to *Violante*, - -	Mr. *Lewis*.
Col. Britton,	A Scotchman, - - - -	Mr. *Smith*.
Gibby,	His Footman, - - - -	Mr. *Shuter*.
Lissardo,	Servant to *Felix*, - - - -	Mr. *Dyer*.

WOMEN.

Donna Violante,	{ Design'd for a Nun by her Father, in Love with *Felix*, }	Miss *Macklyn*.
Donna Isabella,	Sister to *Felix*, - - -	Mrs. *Mattocks*.
Flora,	Her Maid, - - - - -	Mrs. *Pitt*.
Inis,	Maid to *Violante*, - - -	Mrs. *Green*.

Alguzil, Attendants, Servants, &c.

SCENE, *LISBON*.

THE
WONDER.

❈❈❈❈❈❈❈❈❈❈❈❈❈❈❈❈❈❈❈❈❈❈❈❈

ACT I. SCENE I.

Enter Don Lopez *meeting* Frederick.

Fred. MY Lord, *Don Lopez.*

Don Lopez. How d'ye, *Frederick?*

Fred. At your Lordship's Service, I am glad to fee you look fo well, my Lord; I hope *Antonio* is out of Danger.

D. Lop. Quite contrary; his Fever increafes they tell me; and the Surgeons are of Opinion his Wound is mortal.

Fred. Your Son *Don Felix* is fafe, I hope.

D. Lop. I hope fo too, but they offer large Rewards to apprehend him.

Fred. When heard your Lordfhip from him?

D. Lop. Not fince he went; I forbad him writing till the publick News gave him an Account of *Antonio's* Health. Letters might be intercepted, and the Place of his Abode difcovered.

Fred. Your Caution was good, my Lord; tho' I am impatient to hear from *Felix*, yet his Safety is my chief Concern. Fortune has malicioufly ftruck a Bar between us in the Affairs of Life, but fhe has done me the Honour to unite our Souls.

D. Lop. I am not ignorant of the Friendfhip between my Son and you. I have heard him commend your Morals, and lament your Want of noble Birth.

Fred. That's Nature's Fault, my Lord: 'tis fome Comfort not to owe one's Misfortune to one's felf, yet 'tis impoffible not to regret the Want of noble Birth

D. Lop. 'Tis pity indeed fuch excellent Parts as you are Mafter of, fhould be eclipfed by mean Extraction.

Fred. Such Commendation would make me vain, my Lord, did you not caft in the Allay of my Extraction.

D. Lop. There's no Condition of Life without its Cares, and it is the Perfection of a Man to wear 'em as eafy as he can; this unfortunate Duel of my Son's does not pafs without Impreffion. But fince it's paft Prevention,

A 4 all

all my Concern is now, how he may efcape the Punifh-
ment; if *Antonio* dies, *Felix* fhall for *England*. You
have been there; what fort of People are the *Englifh?*

Fred My Lord, the *Englifh* are by Nature, what the
ancient *Romans* were by Difcipline, courageous, bold,
hardy, and in love with Liberty. Liberty is the Idol
of the *Englifh*, under whofe Banner all the Nation lifts;
give but the word for Liberty, and ftraight more arm-
ed Legions would appear, than *France* and *Philip* keep
in conftant Pay

D. Lop I like their Principles; who does not wifh for
Freedom in all Degrees of Life? Tho' common Prudence
fometimes makes us act againft it, as I am now obliged to
do, for I intend to marry my Daughter to *Don Guzman*,
whom I expect from *Holland* every Day, whither he went
to take Poffeffion of a large Eftate left him by his Uncle.

Fred. You will not furely facrifice the lovely *Ifabella*,
to Age, Avarice, and a Fool, pardon the Expreffion,
my Lord, but my Concern for your beauteous Daughter
tranfports me beyond that good Manners which I ought
to pay your Lordfhip's Prefence

D Lop I can't deny the Juftnefs of the Character,
Frederick, but you are not infenfible what I have fuffer-
ed by thefe Wars; and he has two things which render
him very agreeable to me for a Son-in-law, he is rich
and well-born, as for his being a Fool, I don't conceive how that can be any Blot in a Hufband, who is
already poffeffed of a good Eftate.——A poor Fool indeed
is a very fcandalous Thing, and fo are your poor Wits,
in my Opinion, who have nothing to be vain of, but
the Infide of their Skulls: now for *Don Guzman*, I
know I can rule him, as I think fit; this is acting the
politic Part, *Frederick*, without which it is impoffible to
keep up the Port of this Life.

Fred. But have you no Confideration for your Daughter's Welfare, my Lord?

D Lop Is a Hufband of twenty thoufand Crowns a
Year no Confideration? Now I think it a very good
Confideration.

Fred. One way, my Lord. But what will the World
fay of fuch a Match?

D. Lop. Sir, I value not the World a Button.

Fred.

Fred. I cannot think your Daughter can have any Inclination for such a Husband.

D Lop. There I believe you are pretty much in the right, tho' it is a Secret which I never had the Curiosity to inquire into, nor I believe ever shall.——Inclination quotha! Parents would have a fine Time on't if they consulted their Children's Inclinations! I'll venture you a Wager, that in all the Garrison Towns in *Spain* and *Portugal*, during the late War, there were not three Women who have not had an Inclination to every Officer in the whole Army; does it therefore follow, that their Fathers ought to pimp for them? No, no, Sir, it is not a Father's Business to follow his Children's Inclinations till he makes himself a Beggar

Fred. But this is of another Nature, my Lord.

D. Lop. Look ye, Sir, I resolve she shall marry *Don Guzman* the Moment he arrives; tho' I could not govern my Son, I will my Daughter, I assure you

Fred This Match, my Lord, is more preposterous than that which you proposed to your Son, from whence arose this fatal Quarrel —— *Don Antonio*'s Sister, *Elvira*, wanted Beauty only, but *Guzman* every thing, but——

Don. Lop. Money——and that will purchase every thing, and so Adieu. [*Exit.*

Fred. Monstrous! These are the Resolutions which destroy the Comforts of Matrimony——he is rich, and well born, powerful Arguments, indeed! Could I but add them to the Friendship of *Don Felix,* what might I not hope? But a Merchant, and a Grandee of *Spain*, are inconsistent Names——*Lissardo!* From whence came you?

Enter Lissardo *in a Riding Habit.*

Liss That Letter will inform you, Sir.

Fred. I hope your Master's safe.

Liss. I left him so; I have another to deliver which requires Haste—— Your most humble Servant, Sir. [*bowing.*

Fred To *Violante*, I suppose.

Liss. The same. [*Exit.*

Fred (Reads) Dear *Frederick,* the two chief Blessings of this Life, are a Friend, and a Mistress, to be debarred the Sight of those is not to live. I hear nothing of *Antonio*'s Death, and therefore resolve to venture to

thy House this Evening, impatient to see *Violante,* and embrace my Friend.   Yours,   *Felix.*
Pray Heaven he comes undifcover'd.————Ha! Colonel *Britton.*

Enter Colonel Britton *in a Riding Habit.*

Col. *Frederick,* I rejoice to see thee.

Fred. What brought you to *Lisbon,* Colonel?

Col. La Fortune de la Guerre, as the *French* fay I have commanded thefe three laft Years in *Spain,* but my Country has thought fit to ftrike up a Peace, and give us, good *Proteftants,* leave to hope for Chriftian Burial, fo I refolved to take *Lisbon* in my way home.

Fred If you are not provided of a Lodging, Colonel, pray command my Houfe, while you ftay.

Col If I were fure I fhould not be troublefome, I woa'd accept your Offer, *Frederick.*

Fred So far from Trouble, Colonel, I fhall take it as a particular Favour, what have we here?

Col. My Footman; this is our Country Drefs, you muft know, which, for the Honour of *Scotland,* I make all my Servants wear.

Enter Gibby *in a* Highland *Dress*

Gib. What mun I de with the Horfes, and like yer Honour, they will tack cold gin they ftand in the Caufeway.

Fred. Oh! I'll take care of them, what hoa *Vasquez.*

                              [*Enter* Vafquez.

Put thofe Horfes which that honeft Fellow will fhew you, into my Stable, do you hear, and feed them well.

Vaf Yes, Sir ————Sir, by my Mafter's Orders, I am, Sir, your moft obfequious humble Servant. Be pleas'd to lead the Way.

Gib 'Sbleed gang yer gat, Sir, and I fall follow yee: Ife tee hungry to feed on Compliments.   [*Exit*

Fred. Ha, ha, a comical Fellow————Well, how do you like our Country, Colonel?

Col. Why Faith, *Frederick,* a Man might pafs his Time agreeable enough with infide of a Nunnery; but to behold fuch Troops of foft, plump, tender, melting, wifhing, nay willing Girls too, thro' a damn'd Grate, gives us *Priefts* ftrong Temptations to plunder Ah, *Frederick,* your Priefts are wicked Rogues. They im-

                                                        mure

mure Beauty for their own proper Ufe, and fhew it only to the Laity to create Defires, and inflame Accompts, that they may purchafe Pardons at a dearer Rate.

Fred. I own Wenching is fomething more difficult here than in *England*, where Women's Liberties are fubfervient to their Inclinations, and Hufbands feem of no Effect, but to take Care of the Children which their Wives provide.

Col. And does Reftraint get the better of Inclination with your Women here? No, I'll be fworn not even in fourfcore. Don't I know the Conftitution of the *Spanifh* Ladies?

Fred. And of all Ladies where you come, Colonel; you were ever a Man of Gallantry.

Col. Ah, *Frederick*, the *Kirk* half ftarves us *Scotchmen*. We are kept fo fharp at home, that we feed like Cannibals abroad. Hark ye, haft thou never a pretty Acquaintance now that thou would'ft confign over to a Friend for half an Hour, ha?

Fred Faith, Colonel, I am the worft Pimp in *Chriftendom*; you had better truft to your own Luck; the Women will foon find you out, I warrant you.

Col. Ay, but it is dangerous foraging in an Enemy's Country, and fince I have fome Hopes of feeing my own again, I had rather purchafe my Pleafure, than run the Hazard of a *Stilletto* in my Guts 'Egad I think I muft e'en marry, and facrifice my Body for the good of my Soul; wilt thou recommend me to a Wife then, one that is willing to exchange her *Moydores* for *Englifh* Liberty; ha Friend?

Fred She muft be very handfome, I fuppofe.

Col. The handfomer the better———but be fure fhe has a Nofe.

Fred Ay, ay, and fome Gold

Col. Oh, very much Gold, I fhall never be able to fwallow the Matrimonial Pill, if it be not well gilded.

Fred Puh, Beauty will make it flide down nimbly

Col. At firft perhaps it may, but the fecond or third Dofe will choak me———I confefs, *Frederick*, Women are the prettieft Play-things in Nature, but Gold, fubftantial Gold, gives 'em the Air, the Mien, the Shape, the Grace, and Beauty of a Goddefs.

Fred

Fred. And has not Gold the same Divinity in their Eyes, Colonel?

Col. Too often——Money is the very God of Marriage, the Poets dress him in a Saffron Robe, by which they figure out the golden Deity, and his lighted Torch blazons those mighty Charms, which encourage us to list under his Banner

No, marry now for Love, no, that's a Jest ·
The self same Bargain serves for Wife and Beast.

Fred. You are always gay, Colonel; come, shall we take a refreshing Glass at my House, and consider what has been said?

Col. I have two or three Compliments to discharge for some Friends, and then I shall wait on you with Pleasure Where do you live?

Fred. At yon corner House with the green Rails.

Col. In the Close of the Evening I will endeavour to kiss your Hand. Adieu.   [*Exit.*

Fred. I will expect you with Impatience.   [*Exit.*

Enter Isabella *and* Inis *her Maid.*

Inis. For Goodness sake, Madam, where are you going in this Pet?

Isab Any where to avoid Matrimony; the Thoughts of a Husband is as terrible to me as the Sight of a Hobgoblin.

Inis Ay, of an old Husband; but if you may chuse for yourself, I fancy Matrimony would be no such frightful thing to you.

Isab You are pretty much in the right, *Inis*; but to be forc'd into the Arms of an Idiot, a sneaking, sniveling, driviling, avaricious Fool, who has neither Person to please the Eye, Sense to charm the Ear, nor Generosity to supply those Defects. Ah, *Inis!* what pleasant Lives Women lead in *England*, where Duty wears no Fetter but Inclination The Custom of our Country inslaves us from our very Cradles, first to our Parents, next to our Husbands, and when Heaven is so kind to rid us of both these, our Brothers still usurp Authority, and expect a blind Obedience from us, so that Maids, Wives, or Widows, we are little better than Slaves to the Tyrant Man; therefore, to avoid their Power, I resolve to cast myself into a Monastry.

Inis. That is, you'll cut your own Throat to avoid another's doing it for you. Ah, Madam, thofe Eyes tell me you have no Nun's Flefh about you : a Monaftry, quotha ! Where you'll wifh yourfelf into the Green-ficknefs in a Month

Ifab. What care I, there will be no Man to plague me.

Inis. No, nor what's much worfe, to pleafe you neither —Odflife, Madam, you are the firft Woman that e'er defpair'd in a Chriftian Country—Were I in your Place—

Ifab. Why, what would your Wifdom do if you were ?

Inis. I'd embark with the firft fair Wind with all my Jewels, and feek my Fortune on t'other fide the Water ; no Shore can treat you worfe than your own ; there's ne'er a Father in *Chriftendom* fhould make me marry any Man againft my Will.

Ifab I am too great a Coward to follow your Advice, I muft contrive fome way to avoid *Don Guzman*, and yet ftay in my own Country.

Enter Don Lopez.

Lop. Muft you fo, Miftrefs ? but I fhall take Care to prevent you. *(Afide)* *Ifabella*, whither are you going, my Child ?

Ifab Ha ! my Father ! to Church, Sir.

Inis. The old Rogue has certainly over-heard her. [*Afide*

Lop. Your Devotion muft needs be very ftrong, or your Memory very weak, my Dear ; why Vefpers are over for this Night ; come, come, you fhall have a better Errand to Church than to fay your Prayers there. *Don Guzman* is arriv'd in the River, and I expect him afhore To-morrow.

Ifab. Ha, To-morrow !

Lop. He writes me Word, That his Eftate in *Holland* is worth 12000 Crowns a Year, which, together with what he had before, will make thee the happieft Wife in *Lifbon.*

Ifab And the moft unhappy Woman in the World. Oh Sir ! If I have any Power in your Heart, if the Tendernefs of a Father be not quite extinct, hear me with Patience.

Lop. No Objection againft the Marriage, and I will hear whatfoever thou haft to fay.

Ifab. That's torturing me on the Rack, and forbidding

me

me to groan; upon my Knees I claim the Privilege of Flesh and Blood. - [*Kneels.*

Lop. I grant it, thou shalt have an Arm full of Flesh and Blood To-morrow; Flesh and Blood, quotha· Heaven forbid I should deny thee Flesh and Blood, my Girl.

Inis. Here's an old Dog for you. [*Aside.*

Isab Do not mistake, Sir; the fatal Stroke which separates Soul and Body, is not more terrible to the Thoughts of Sinners, than the Name of *Guzman* to my Ear.

Lop Puh, puh; you lye, you lye

Isab My frighted Heart beats hard against my Breast, as if it sought a Passage to your Feet, to beg you'd change your Purpose.

Lop A very pretty Speech this; if it were turn'd into blank Verse, it would serve for a *Tragedy*, why, thou hast more Wit than I thought thou hadst, Child. —— I fancy this was all *extempore*, I don't believe thou did'st ever think one Word on't before.

Inis. Yes, but she has, my Lord, for I have heard her say the same things a thousand Times.

Lop How, how ? What do you top your second-hand Jests upon your Father, Hussy, who knows better what's good for you than you do yourself ? remember 'tis your Duty to obey. ·

Isab. (Rising) I never disobey'd before, and wish I had not Reason now; but Nature has got the better of my Duty, and makes me loathe the harsh Commands you lay.

Lop Ha, ha, very fine ! Ha, ha

Isab. Death itself would be more welcome.

Lop Are you sure of that ?

Isab. I am your Daughter, my Lord, and can boast as strong a Resolution as yourself, I'll die before I'll marry *Guzman.*

Lop. Say you so ? I'll try that presently (*Draws.*) Here, let me see with what Dexterity you can breathe a Vein now (*offers her his Sword*) The Point is pretty sharp, 'twill do your Business, I warrant you

Inis. Bless me, Sir, What do you mean to put a Sword into the Hands of a desperate Woman ·

Lop Desperate, ha, ha, ha, you see how desperate she is , what art thou frighted, little *Bell* ? ha !

Isab. I confess, I am startled at your Morals, Sir

Lop.

Lop. Ay, ay, Child, thou hadſt better take the Man, he'll hurt thee the leaſt of the two.

Iſab. I ſhall take neither, Sir; Death has many Doors, and when I can live no longer with Pleaſure, I ſhall find one to let him in at without your Aid.

Lop. Say'ſt thou ſo, my dear *Bell?* Ods, I'm afraid thou art a little Lunatick, *Bell.* I muſt take care of thee, Child, *(takes hold of her, and pulls out of his Pocket a Key)* I ſhall make bold to ſecure thee, my Dear · I'll ſee if Locks and Bars can keep thee till *Guzman* come ; go, get into your Chamber.

There I'll your boaſted Reſolution try,
And ſee who'll get the better, you or I.
(puſhes her in and locks the Door.

ACT II.

Scene, *a Room in* Don Pedro's *Houſe.*

Enter Donna Violante *reading a Letter, and* Flora *following.*

Flora. WHAT, muſt that Letter be read again?

Vio. Yes, and again, and again, and again, a thouſand Times again ; a Letter from a faithful Lover can ne'er be read too often , it ſpeaks ſuch kind, ſuch ſoft, ſuch tender Things——————[*Kiſſes it.*

Flo. But always the ſame Language

Vio It does not charm the leſs for that.

Flo. In my Opinion nothing charms that does not change ; and any Compoſition of the four and twenty Letters, after the firſt Eſſay, from the ſame Hand, muſt be dull, except a Bank Note, or a Bill of Exchange

Vio Thy Taſte is my Averſion—— *(Reads)* My all that's charming, ſince Life's not Life exil'd from thee, this Night ſhall bring me to thy Arms. *Frederick* and thee are all I truſt Theſe ſix Weeks Abſence has been in Love's Accompt ſix hundred Years ; when it is dark, expect the wonted Signal at thy Window, till when, adieu, thine more than his own. *Felix*

Flo Who would not have ſaid as much to a Lady of her Beauty, and twenty thouſand Pounds —— Were I a Man, methinks, I could have ſaid a hundred finer Things ;

Things;

Things; I would have compar'd your Eyes to the Stars, your Teeth to Ivory, your Lips to Coral, your Neck to Alabaster, your Shape to——

Vio No more of your Bombast, Truth is the best Eloquence in a Lover——What Proof remains ungiven of his Love? When his Father threatned to disinherit him, for refusing *Don Antonio*'s Sister, from whence sprung this unhappy Quarrel, did it shake his Love for me? And now, tho' strict Enquiry runs thro' every Place, with large Rewards to apprehend him, does he not venture all for me?

Flo But you know, Madam, your Father *Don Pedro* designs you for a Nun, and says your Grandfather left you your Fortune upon that Condition.

Vio. Not without my Approbation, Girl, when I come to One and Twenty, as I am informed. But however, I shall run the Risk of that, go, call in *Lissardo*

Flo Yes, Madam; now for a Thousand Verbal Questions.   [*Exit, and re-enter with* Lissardo.

Vio Well, and how do you do, *Lissardo?*

Liss. Ah, very weary, Madam——Faith thou look'st wondrous pretty, *Flora.*   [*Aside to* Flora.

Vio How came you?

Liss En Chevalier, Madam, upon a Hackney Jade, which they told me formerly belong'd to an *English* Colorel But I should have rather thought she had been bred a good *Roman Catholick* all her Life-time; for she down on her Knees to every Stock and Stone we came along by. —— My Chops water for a Kiss, they do, *Flora*   [*Aside to* Flora.

Flo. You'd make one believe you are wond'rous fond now.

Vio. Where did you leave your Master?

Liss Od, f I had you alone, House-Wife, I'd show you how fond I cou'd be——[*Aside to* Flora.]At a little Farm-House, Madam, about five Miles off; he'll be at *Don Frederick*'s in the Evening——Od, I will so revenge my self of those Lips of thine   [*To* Flora.

Vio. Is he in Health?

Flo Oh, you counterfeit wonderous well [*To* Lissardo.

Liss. No, every Body knows I counterfeit very ill
    [*To* Flora.

Vio How say you? Is *Felix* ill? What's his Distemper? Ha!   *Liss.*

Liſſ A pies on't, I hate to be interrupted——Love, Madam, Love —— In ſhort, Madam, I believe he has thought of nothing but your Ladyſhip ever ſince he left *Liſbon.* I am ſure he cou'd not, if I may judge of his Heart by my own. [*Looking lovingly upon* Flora.

Vio. How came you ſo well acquainted with your Maſter's Thoughts, *Liſſardo?*

Liſſ. By an infallible Rule, Madam ; Words are the Pictures of the Mind, you know ; now to prove he thinks of nothing but you, he talks of nothing but you —— for Example, Madam, coming from Shooting t'other Day, with a Brace of Partridges, *Liſſardo,* ſaid he, go bid the Cook roaſt me theſe *Violante's* —— I flew into the Kitchen, full of Thoughts of thee, cry'd, Here, Cook, roaſt me theſe *Florella's.* [*To* Flora.

Flo Ha, ha, excellent—— You mimick your Maſter then it ſeems

Liſſ I can do every thing as well as my Maſter, you little Rogue —— Another Time, Madam, the Prieſt came to make him a Viſit, he call'd out haſtily, *Liſſardo,* ſaid he, bring a *Violante* for my Father to ſit down on ; —— then he often miſtook my Name, Madam, and call'd me *Violante ;* in ſhort, I heard it ſo often, that it became as familiar to me as my Prayers.

Vio You live very merrily then it ſeems.

Liſſ Oh, exceeding merry, Madam [*Kiſſes* Flora's *Hand.*

Vio Ha ! exceeding merry ; had you Treats and Balls?

Liſſ. Oh ! Yes, yes, Madam, ſeveral.

Flo You are mad, *Liſſardo,* you don't mind what my Lady ſays to you. [*Aſide to* Liſſardo.

Vio. Ha ! Balls —— Is he ſo merry in my Abſence ? And did your Maſter dance, *Liſſardo ?*

Liſſ. Dance, Madam ! Where, Madam ?

Vio Why, at thoſe Balls you ſpeak of.

Liſſ Balls ! What Balls, Madam ?

Vio. Why, ſure you are in Love, *Liſſardo ;* did not you ſay, but now, you had Balls where you have been ?

Liſſ Balls, Madam ! Odſlife, I aſk your Pardon, Madam ! I, I, I, had miſlaid ſome Waſh-Balls of my Maſter's, t'other Day ; and becauſe I cou'd not think where I had laid them, juſt when he aſk'd for them, he very fairly broke my Head, Madam, and now it ſeems

I can

I can think of nothing elfe. Alas! He dance, Madam ' No, no, poor Gentleman, he is as melancholy as an unbraced Drum.

Vio Poor *Felix* ! There, wear that Ring for your Mafter's Sake, and let him know I fhall be ready to receive him.   *[Exit* Vio.

Liff. I fhall, Madam — *(puts on the Ring.)* methinks a Diamond Ring is a vaft Addition to the little Finger of a Gentleman.   *[admiring his Hand.*

Flo That Ring muft be mine————Well, *Liffardo !* What Hafte you make to pay off Arrears now ? Look how the Fellow ftands '

Liff. Egad, methinks I have a very pretty Hand—— and very white,——and the Shape ! ——Faith I never minded it fo much before ! ——— In my Opinion it is a very fine fhaped Hand —— and becomes a Diamond Ring, as well as the firft Grandee's in *Portugal.*

Flo. The Man's tranfported ' Is this your Love! This your Impatience !

Liff. *(Takes Snuff)* Now in my Mind ———I take Snuff with a very *Jantee* Air —— Well, I am perfuaded I want nothing but a Coach and a Title, to make me a very fine Gentleman.   *(Struts about.*

Flo. Sweet Mr. *Liffardo,* *(curtefying)* If I may prefume to fpeak to you, without affronting your little Finger——

Liff Odfo, Madam, I afk your Pardon — Is it to me, or to the Ring——you direct your Difcourfe, Madam ?

Flo. Madam ! Good lack ' How much a Diamond Ring improves one !

Liff. Why, tho' I fay it—I can carry myfelf as well as any Body—But what wer't thou going to fay, Child ?

Flo. Why I was going to fay, that I fancy you had beft let me keep that Ring ; it will be a very pretty Wedding-Ring, *Liffardo,* would it not ?

Liff. Humph ' Ah ! But—— but —— but——I be-lieve I fhan't marry yet awhile.

Flo You fhan't, you fay,—— Very well ! I fuppofe you defign that Ring for *Inis.*

Liff. No, no, I never bribe an old Acquaintance — Perhaps I might let it fparkle in the Eyes of a Stranger a little, till we come to a right Underftanding—— But then, like all other mortal Things, it would return from whence it came.   *Flo.*

Flo. Infolent——Is that your Manner of dealing ?

Liff. With all but thee ——Kifs me you little Rogue you.. *(Hugging her.*

Flo. Little Rogue ! prithee Fellow, don't be fo familiar, *(pufhing him away.)* if I mayn't keep your Ring, I can keep my Kifses.

Liff. You can you fay ! Spoke with the Air of a Chamber-maid.

Flo Reply'd with the Spirit of a ferving Man.

Liff Prithee, *Flora*, don't let you and I fall out, I am in a merry Humour, and fhall certainly fall in fomewhere.

Flo. What care I, where you fall in.

Enter Violante.

Vio. Why do you keep *Liffardo* fo long, *Flora* ? When you don't know how foon my Father may awake, his Afternoon Naps are never long.

Flo. Had *Don Felix* been with her, fhe would not have thought the Time long ; thefe Ladies confider no Body's Wants but their own. *[Afide.*

Vio. Go, go, let him out, and bring a Candle.

Flo. Yes, Madam.

Liff. I fly, Madam. *[Exit Liff and* Flora.

Vio. The Day draws in, and Night, ——the Lover's Friend advances —— Night more welcome than the Sun to me, becaufe it brings my Love.

Flo *(Shrieks within.)* Ah Thieves, Thieves ! Murder, Murder !

Vio *(Shrieks)* Ah ! defend me Heaven ! What do I hear ? *Felix* is certainly purfu'd, and will be taken.

Enter Flora *running*

Vio. How now ! why doft ftare fo ? Anfwer me quickly ! What's the Matter ?

Flo Oh, Madam ! as I was letting out *Liffardo*, a Gentleman rufhed between him and I, ftruck down my Candle, and is bringing a dead Perfon in his Arms into our Houfe.

Vio. Ha ! a dead Perfon ! Heav'n grant it does not prove my *Felix*.

Flo. Here they are, Madam.

Enter Colonel *with* Ifabella *in his Arms.*

Vio. I'll retire till you difcover the Meaning of the Accident. *[Exit.*

Col.

Col. (*Sets* Isabella *down in a Chair, and addresses himself to* Flora.)

Madam, The Necessity this Lady was under, of being conveyed into some House with Speed and Secresy, will, I hope, excuse any Indecency I might be guilty of, in pressing so rudely into this ——I am an entire Stranger to her Name and Circumstances, would I were so to her Beauty too [*Aside*] I commit her, Madam, to your Care, and fly to make her Retreat secure, if the Street be clear, permit me to return, and learn from her own Mouth, if I can be farther serviceable. Pray, Madam, how is the Lady of this House call'd?

Flo. Violante, Senior ——He is a handsome *Cavalier,* and promises well.   [*Aside.*

Col Are you she, Madam?

Flo Only her Woman, *Senior*

Col Your humble Servant, Mrs. Pray be careful of the Lady ———— (*gives her two Moydores*) [*Exit* Col.

Flo. Two Moydores! Well, he is a generous Fellow. This is the only Way to make one careful; I find all Countries understand the Constitution of a Chambermaid.

Enter Violante.

Vio. Was you distracted, *Flora?* To tell my Name to a Man you never saw! Unthinking Wench! Who knows what this may turn to — What is the Lady dead! Ah! defend me Heaven, 'tis *Isabella,* Sister to my *Felix,* what has befallen her? Pray Heaven he's safe. — Run and fetch some cold Water. [*Exit* Flora, *and enters with Water.*] *Isabella,* Friend, speak to me, Oh! speak to me, or I shall die with Apprehension.

Flo See, she revives.

Isab. O! hold, my dearest Father, do not force me, indeed I cannot love him.

Vio. How wild she talks. ————

Isab Ha! where am I?

Vio. With one as sensible of thy Pain as thou thy self can'st be.

Isab Violante! What kind Star preserved, and lodg'd me here?

Flo It was a Terrestrial Star, call'd a Man, Madam; pray *Jupiter* he proves a lucky one.

Isab.

Isab. Oh! I remember now, forgive me, dear *Violante*, my Thoughts ran so much upon the Danger I escap'd, I forgot.

Vio. May I not know your Story?

Isab. Thou art no Stranger to one part of it; I have often told thee that my Father design'd to sacrifice me to the Arms of *Don Guzman*, who it seems is just return'd from *Holland*, and expected ashore to-morrow, the Day that he has set to celebrate our Nuptials. Upon my refusing to obey him, he lock'd me into my Chamber, vowing to keep me there till he arriv'd, and force me to consent. I know my Father to be positive, never to be won from his Design, and having no hope left me, to escape the Marriage, I leap'd from the Window, into the Street.

Vio. You have not hurt yourself, I hope.

Isab No, a Gentleman passing by, by Accident, caught me in his Arms; at first my Fright made me apprehend it was my Father, till he assured me to the contrary.

Flor He is a very fine Gentleman, I promise you, Madam, and a well-bred Man, I warrant him. I think I never saw a Grandee put his Hand into his Pocket with a better Air in my whole Life-time; then he open'd his Purse with such a Grace, that nothing but his Manner of presenting me the Gold cou'd equal

Vio There is but one common Road to the Heart of a Servant, and 'tis impossible for a generous Person to mistake it.——But how came you hither, *Isabella?*

Isab I know not; I desired the Stranger to convey me to the next *Monastry*, but ere I reach'd the Door, I saw, or fancy'd that I saw, *Lissardo*, my Brother's Man, and the Thought that his Master might not be far off, flung me into a Swoon, which is all that I remember: Ha! What's here [*takes up a Letter*] For Colonel *Britton*, *to be left at the Post-House in* Lisbon; this must be brought by the Stranger which brought me hither.

Vio. Thou art fallen into the Hands of a Soldier, take care he does not lay thee under Contribution, Girl.

Isab. I find he is a Gentleman; and if he is but unmarried, I could be content to follow him all the World over. —But I shall never see him more I fear [*Sighs and pauses.*

Vio. What makes you sigh, *Isabella?*

Isab.

Isab. The Fear of falling into my Father's Clutches again.

Vio Can I be serviceable to you?

Isab Yes, if you conceal me two or three Days.

Vio. You command my House and Secresy.

Isab. I thank you, *Violante.* ——— I wish you would oblige me with Mrs *Flora* awhile.

Vio. I'll send for her to you—I must watch if Dad be still asleep, or here will be no Room for *Felix.*   [*Exit.*

Isab. Well, I don't know what ails me, methinks I wish I could find this Stranger out.

Enter Flora.

Flo. Does your Ladyship want me, Madam?

Isab. Ay, Mrs. *Flora*, I resolve to make you my Confident.

Flo. I shall endeavour to discharge my Duty, Madam.

Isab. I doubt it not, and desire you to accept this as a Token of my Gratitude.

Flo. O dear *Seniora*, I should have been your humble Servant without a Fee:

Isab. I believe it ——— But to the Purpose——Do you think if you saw the Gentleman which brought me hither, you shou'd know him again.

Flo. From a Thousand, Madam; I have an excellent Memory where an handsome Man is concerned; when he went away he said he would return again immediately.   I admire he comes not.

Isab. Here, did you say? You rejoice me ——— Tho' I'll not see him if he comes : cou'd not you contrive to give him a Letter?

Flo. With the Air of a Duenna ———

Isab. Not in this House——you must veil and follow him——He must not know it comes from me.

Flo. What do you take me for a Novice in Love Affairs? Tho' I have not practis'd the Art since I have been in *Donna Violante*'s Service, yet I have not lost the Theory of a Chamber-maid — Do you write the Letter, and leave the rest to me ——— Here, here, here's Pen, Ink, and Paper.

Isab. I'll do it in a Minute.   *(Sits down to write.*

Flo. So! this is a Business after my own Heart; Love always takes care to reward his Labourers, and

Great-

Great-Britain feems to be his favourite Country —Oh, I long to fee the other two Moydores with a *British* Air ——Methinks there's a Grace peculiar to that Nation in making a Prefent.

Ifab. So I have done, now if he does but find this Houfe again!

Flo. If he fhould not——I warrant I'll find him if he's in *Lifbon.* (*Puts the Letter into her Bofom.*
                    Enter Violante.

Vio *Flora*, watch my Papa, he's faft afleep in his Study—If you find him ftir give me Notice.—Hark, I hear *Felix* at the Window, admit him inftantly, and then to your Poft. [*Exit* Flora.

Ifab. What fay you, *Violante?* Is my Brother come?

Vio. It is his Signal at the Window.

Ifab. (*Kneels*) Oh! *Violante*, I conjure thee by all the Love thou bear'ft to *Felix*——By thy own generous Nature—Nay more by that unfpotted Virtue thou art Miftrefs of, do not difcover to my Brother I am here.

Vio. Contrary to your Defire, be affur'd I never fhall. But where's the Danger?

Ifab Art thou born in *Lifbon*, and afk that Queftion? He'll think his Honour blemifh'd by my Difobedience, and would reftore me to my Father, or kill me; therefore, dear, dear Girl.

Vio. Depend upon my Friendfhip, nothing fhall draw the Secret from thefe Lips, not even *Felix*, tho' at the Hazard of his Love, I hear him coming, retire into that Clofet.

Ifab Remember, *Violante*, upon thy Promife my very Life depends. [*Exit.*

Vio. When I betray thee, may I fhare thy Fate.
                    Enter Flora *and* Felix.

Vio. My *Felix*, my everlafting Love. (*runs into his Arms.*

Fel. My Life, my Soul! my *Violante!*

Vio. What Hazards doft thou run for me? Oh, how fhall I requite thee?

Fel. If during this tedious painful Exile, thy Thoughts have never wander'd from thy *Felix*, thou has made me more than Satisfaction.

Vio. Can there be Room within this Heart for any but thyfelf? No, if the God of Love were loft to all the reft of Human Kind, thy Image wou'd fecure him
                                                in

in my Breaſt; I am all Truth, all Love, all Faith, and know no jealous Fears.

Fel. My Heart's the proper Sphere where Love reſides; could he quit that, he wou'd be no where found; and yet, *Violante,* I'm in doubt.

Vio. Did I ever give thee Cauſe to doubt, my *Felix?*

Fel. True Love has many Fears, and Fear as many Eyes as Fame; yet ſure I think they ſee no Fault in thee —What's that? (*the Colonel pats at the Window without.*

Vio. What? I heard nothing.　　　　(*He pats again.*

Fel. Ha! What means this Signal at your Window?

Vio. Somebody, perhaps, in paſſing by, might accidentally hit it, it can be nothing elſe

Col. (*Within*) Hiſt, hiſt, *Donna Violante, Donna Violante.*

Fel. They uſe your Name by Accident too, do they, Madam?　　　　　　　　　　　　[*Enter* Flora.

Flo There is a Gentleman at the Window, Madam, which I fancy to be him who brought *Iſabella* hither; ſhall I admit him?　　　　　　(*Aſide to* Violante.

Vio. Admit Diſtraction rather, thou art the Cauſe of this, unthinking Wretch!

Fel. What has Mrs. *Scout* brought you freſh Intelligence? Death, I'll know the Bottom of this immediately!　　　　　　　　　　　　(*Offers to go.*

Flo. Scout! I ſcorn your Words, *Senior.*

Vio. Nay, nay, nay, you muſt not leave me.
　　　　　　　　(*Runs and catches hold of him.*

Fel. Oh! 'Tis not fair, not to anſwer the Gentleman, Madam. It is none of his Fault, that his Viſit proves unſeaſonable, pray let me go, my Preſence is but a Reſtraint upon you.　　(*Struggles to get from her.*
　　　　　　　　　　(*The Colonel pats again.*

Vio. Was ever Accident ſo miſchievous!　　[*Aſide.*

Flo. It muſt be the Colonel; now to deliver my Letter to him.　　　　　　　　　　　　[*Exit.*

Fel. Hark! he grows impatient at your Delay—Why do you hold the Man, whoſe Abſence wou'd oblige you? Pray let me go, Madam; conſider, the Gentleman wants you at the Window, Confuſion! (*Struggles ſtill.*

Vio. It is not me he wants.

Fel. Death, not you? Is there another of your Name in the Houſe? But, come on, convince me of the Truth of what you ſay: Open the Window, if his Buſineſs

finefs does not lie with you, your Converfation may be
heard ——This, and only this, can take off my Sufpicion——What do you paufe! Oh! Guilt! Guilt! Have
I caught you? Nay then I'll leap the Balcony, If I remember, this Way leads to it   *(breaks forth, and
                              goes to the Door where Ifabella is.)*

Vio. Oh Heaven! What fhall I do now, hold, hold,
hold, hold, not for the World——You enter there
——Which way fhall I preferve his Sifter from his
Knowledge?   *(Ʈʋ̃*

Fel. What have I touch'd you? do you fear your
Lover's Life?

Vio. I fear for none but you——For Goodnefs Sake,
do not fpeak fo loud, my *Felix* If my Father hear you
I am loft for ever, that Door opens into his Apartment.
What fhall I do if he enters? There he finds his Sifter
——If he goes out he'll quarrel with the Stranger——
Nay do not ftruggle to be gone, my *Felix*——If I open
the Window he may difcover the whole Intrigue, and
yet of all Evils we ought to chufe the leaft. Your Curi-
ofity fhall be fatisfied Whoe'er you are that with fuch In-
folence dare ufe my Name, and give the Neighbour-
hood Pretence to reflect upon my Conduct, I charge you
inftantly to be gone, or expect the Treatment you deferve
          (goes to the Window and throws up the Safh.

Col. I afk Pardon, Madam, and will obey, but
when I left this Houfe to Night——

Fel. Good.

Vio. It is moft certainly the Stranger; what will be
the Event of this Heaven knows. *(Afide.)* You are
miftaken in the Houfe, I fuppofe, Sir.

Fel. No, no, he is not miftaken——Pray, Madam,
let the Gentleman go on.

Vio. Wretched Misfortune, pray be gone, Sir, I know
of no Bufinefs you have here

Col. I wifh I did not know it neither ——But this
Houfe contains my Soul, then can you blame my Body
for hovering about it

Fel. Excellent!

Vio. Dull action! He will infallibly difcover Ifa——
I tell you again you are miftaken, however, for your
own Satisfaction call To morrow

Fel.

Fel Matchlefs Impudence! An Affignation before my Face—No, he fhall not live to meet your Wifhes.
(Takes out a Piftol and goes towards the Window, fhe catches hold of him.

Vio Ah! *(Shrieks)* hold I conjure you

Col To-morrow's an Age, Madam! May I not be admitted to night?

Vio. If you be a Gentleman I command your Abfence. Unfortunate! What will my Stars do with me?
[Afide.

Col I have done——Only this——Be careful of my Life, for it is in your keeping. *(Exit from the Window*

Fel. Pray obferve the Gentleman's Requeft, Madam
(Walking off from her

Vio I am all Confufion.   *(Afide.*

Fel You are all Truth, all Love, all Faith· Oh thou all Woman!————How have I been deceiv'd? S'Death, cou'd you not have impos'd upon me for this one Night? Cou'd neither my faithful Love, nor the Hazard I have run to fee you, make me worthy to be cheated on

Vio Can I bear this from you?   *(Weeps.*

Fel. *(Repeats)* When I left this Houfe to-night——'To-night, the Devil! Return fo foon!

Vio Oh *Ifabella!* What haft thou involv'd me in *(Afide.*

Fel. *(Repeats)* This Houfe contains my Sou

Vio Yet I refolve to keep the Secret.   *(Afide.*

Fel *(Repeats)* Be careful of my Life, for 'tis in your keeping ——Damnation! ——How ugly fhe appears!
(Looking at her

Vio. Do not look fo fternly on me, but believe me, *Felix,* I have not injur'd you, nor am I falfe

Fel Not falfe, not injur'd me! Oh *Violante,* loft and abandoned to thy Vice! Not falfe, oh monftrous!

Vio. Indeed I am not——There is a Caufe which I muft not reveal——Oh think how far Honour can oblige your Sex————Then allow a Woman may be bound by the fame Rule to keep a Secret.

Fel Honour, what haft thou to do with Honour, thou that canft admit Plurality of Lovers? A Secret! Ha, ha, ha, his Affairs are wondrous fafe, who trufts his Secret to a Woman's keeping, but you need give yourfelf no

Trouble

Trouble about clearing this Point, Madam, for you are become so indifferent to me, that your Truth and Falshood are the same!

 Vio. My Love!   [*Offers to take his Hand.*
 Fel. My Torment!   [*Turns from her.*
      Enter Flora.

 Flo. So I have deliver'd my Letter to the Colonel, and receiv'd my Fee. [*Aside*] Madam, your Father bade me see what Noise that was—For Goodness sake, Sir, why do you speak so loud!

 Fel. I understand my Cue, Mistress; my Absence is necessary, I'll oblige you. [*going*] [*takes hold of him.*

 Vio. Oh let me undeceive you first!

 Fel Impossible!

 Vio. 'Tis very possible if I durst.

 Fel. Durst! Ha, ha, ha, durst, quotha?

 Vio But another Time I'll tell thee all.

 Fel. Nay, now or never————

 Vio. Now it cannot be.

 Fel. Then it shall never be—Thou most ungrateful of thy Sex, farewel. [*Breaks from her and Exit*

 Vio. Oh exquisite Trial of my Friendship! Yet not even this, shall draw the Secret from me.

 That I'll preserve, let Fortune frown or smile,
 And trust to Love, my Love to reconcile. [*Exit.*

ACT III.
Enter Don Lopez.

Lop. WAS ever Man thus plagu'd! Odsheart, I cou'd swallow my Dagger for Madness; I know not what to think; sure *Frederick* had no Hand in her Escape—She must get out of the Window; and she could not do that without a Ladder; and who cou'd bring it her, but him? Ay, it must be so. The Dislike he shew'd to *Don Guzman* in our Discourse to Day, confirms my Suspicion, and I will charge him home with it, sure Children were given me for a Curse! Why, what innumerable Misfortunes attend us Parents, when we have employed our whole Care to educate, and bring our Children up to Years of Maturity? Just when we expect to reap the Fruits of our Labour, a Man shall, in the tinkling of a Bell, see one hang'd, t'other

     B 2   whor'd

woor'd—This graceless Baggage—But I'll to *Frederick*
immediately, I'll take the *Alguazile* with me and search
his House, and if I find her, I'll use her————by St.
Anthony, I don't know how I'll use her.   *[Exit.*

The Scene changes to the Street.

Enter Colonel *with* Isabella's *Letter in his Hand, and*
Gibby *following.*

Col. Well, tho' I cou'd not see my fair *Incognita*,
Fortune, to make me amends, has flung another Intrigue in my way. Oh! how I love these pretty, kind,
coming Females, that wont give a Man the Trouble of
racking his Invention to deceive them. —Oh *Portugal!*
thou dear Garden of Pleasure————where Love drops
down his mellow Fruit, and every Bough bends to our
Hands, and seems to cry, Come, Pull and Eat; how
deliciously a Man lives here without fear of the Stool
of Repentance? — This Letter I receiv'd from a Lady
in a Veil————Some *Duenna!* Some necessary Imple-
ment of *Cupid!* I suppose the Stile is frank and easy,
I hope like her that writ it. [*Reads*] " Sir, I have seen
" your Person, and like it"————*Very concise*———— ' And
" if you'll meet at five o'Clock in the Morning upon
" the *Terrero de passa*, half an Hour's Conversation
" will let me into your Mind. —" *Ha, ha, ha, a philosophical Wench This is the first Time I ever knew a Woman had any business with the Mind of a Man* ———— " If
" your Intellects answer your outward Appearance, the
" Adventure may not displease you I expect you'll
" not attempt to see my Face, nor offer any thing un-
" becoming the Gentleman I take you for '————
Humph, the Gentleman she takes me for, I hope she
takes me to be Flesh and Blood, and then I am sure I
shall do nothing unbecoming a Gentleman. Well, if I
must not see her Face, it shall go hard if I don't know
where she lives ———— *Gibby.*

Gib Here, an like yer honour

Col Follow me at a good Distance, do you hear
Gibby?

Gib In troth dee I, weel eneugh, Sir

Col I am to meet a—— upon the *Terrero de passa.*

Gib The Deel an mine Eya gin I lern her, Sir

Col. But you will when you come there, Sirrah.

Gib. Like eneugh, Sir, I have as sharp an Eyn till a bony Lass, as ere a Lad in aw *Scotland*; and what man I ate wi' her, Sir?

Col Why, if she and I part, you must watch her home and bring me word where she lives

Gib In troth sal I, Sir, gin the Deel tak her not

Col. Come along then, 'tis pretty near the Time—I like a Woman that rises early to pursue her Inclination.

Thus we improve the Pleasures of the Day,
Whilst tasteless Mortals sleep their Time away [*Exit.*

Scene changes to Frederick's House.

Enter Inis *and* Liffardo

Liff Your Lady run away, and you know not whither say you?

Inis She never greatly car'd for me after finding you and I together, but you are very grave, methinks, Liffardo

Liff [*Looking on the Ring*] Not at all—I have some Thoughts indeed of altering my Course of living; there is a critical Minute in every Man's Life, which if he can but lay hold of, he may make his Fortune.

Inis Ha! What, do I see a Diamond Ring! Where the Duce had he that Ring? You have got a very pretty Ring there, *Liffardo.*

Liff. Aye, the Trifle is pretty enough —But the Lady which gave it to me is a *Bona Roba* in Beauty, I assure you. [*Cocks his Hat and struts.*

Inis I can't bear this—The Lady! What Lady, pray?

Liff Oh fye! There's a Question to ask a Gentleman.

Inis A Gentleman! Why the Fellow's spoil'd! Is this your Love for me? Ungrateful Man, you'll break my Heart, so you will. [*Bursts into Tears.*

Liff Poor tender-hearted Fool ——

Inis If I knew who gave you that Ring, I'd tear her Eyes out, so I wou'd. [*Sobs.*

Liff So, now the Jade wants a little Coaxing why, what dost thou weep for now, my Dear? Ha!

Inis I suppose *Flora* gave you that Ring; but I'll—

Liff. No, the Devil take me if she did, you make

B 3 me

me fwear now—So, they are All for the Ring, but I shall bob 'em: I did but joke, the Ring is none of mine, it is my Mafter's; I am to give it to be new fet, that's all; therefore prithee dry thy Eyes, and kifs me, come.   [*Enter* Flora.

Fra. And do you really fpeak Truth now?

Lifs. Why, do you doubt it?

Flo. So, fo, very well! I thought there was an Intrigue between him and *Ins,* for all he has forfworn it fo often   [*Afide.*

Ins Nor han't you feen *Flora* fince you came to Town.

Flo. Ha! How dares fhe name my Name?   [*Afide.*

Lifs. No, by this Kifs I han't.   [*Kiffes her*

Flo. Here's a difembling Varlet.   [*Afide*

Ins Nor don't you love her at all?

Lifs. Love the Devil, why did not I always tell thee fhe was my Averfion?

Flo. Did you fo, Villain![*Strikes him a Box on the Ear.*

Lifs. Zounds, fhe here! I have made a fine Spot of Work on't.   [*Afide.*

Ins. What's that for? Ha   [*Brufhes up to her.*

Flo. I fhall tell you by and by, Mrs. *Frippery,* if you don't get about your Bufinefs

Ins. Who do you call *Frippery,* Mrs *Trolup?* Pray get about your Bufinefs. If you go to that, I hope you pretend to no Right and Title here

Lifs. What the Devil do they take me for, an Acre of Land, that they quarrel about Right and Title to me?   [*Afide.*

Flo. Pray what Right have you, Miftrefs, to afk that Queftion?

Ins. No matter for that, I can fhew a better Title to him than you, I believe

Flo. What, has he given thee nine Months earneft for a living Title? Ha, ha.

Ins. Don't fling your flaunting Jefts at me, Mis *Boniface,* for I won't take 'em, I affure you

Lifs. So! now am I as great as the fam'd *Alexander* but my dear *Statira* and *Roxana,* don't exert yourfelves fo much about me: Now I fancy, if you wou'd agree lovingly together, I might, in a modeft Way, fatisfy both your Demands upon me.   *Flo.*

Flo. You fatisfy ! No, Sirrah, I am not to be fatisfy d fo foon as you think, perhaps.

Inis. No, nor I neither. —— What do you make no Difference between us ?

Flo. You pitiful Fellow you ; what you fancy, I warrant, that I gave myfelf the Trouble of dogging you, out of Love to your filthy Perfon, but you are miftaken, Sirrah——It was to detect your Treachery —— How often have you fworn to me that you hated *Inis,* and only carried fair for the good Chear fhe gave you ; but that you could never like a Woman with crooked Legs, you faid.

Inis. How, how, Sirrah, crooked Legs ! Ods, I cou'd find in my Heart. *[Snatching up her Petticoat a little.*

Lif. Here's a lying young Jade now ! Prithee, my Dear, moderate thy Paffion *[Coaxingly.*

Inis. I'd have you to know, Sirrah, my Legs was never — your Mafter, I hope, underftands Legs better than you do, Sirrah. *[paffionately*

Lif. My Mafter ! fo, fo. *[Shaking his Head and [winking.*

Flo. I am glad I have done fome Mifchief, however. *[Afide.*

Lif. [*To Inis*] Art thou really fo foolifh to mind what an enrag'd Woman fays ! Don't you fee fhe does it on purpofe to part you and I ? [*runs to* Flora] Cou'd not you find the Joke without putting yourfelf in a Paffion ! You filly Girl you ; why I faw you follow us plain enough, mun, and faid all this, that you might not go back with only your Labour for your Pains—— But you are a revengeful young Slut tho', I tell you that, but come kifs, and be Friends.

Flo. Don't think to coax me ; hang your Kifes

Fel. [*Within*] Liffardo.

Lif. Odfheart, here's my Mafter, the Devil take both thefe Jades for me, what fhall I do with them ?

Inis. Ha ! 'Tis *Don Felix*'s Voice ; I wou'd not have him find me here, with his Footman, for the World. *[Afide.*

Fel. [*Within*] Why Liffardo, Liffardo !

Lif. Coming, Sir. What a Pox will you do ?

Flo. Blefs me, which Way fhall I get out

Lif.

Liss. Nay, nay, you muſt e'en ſet your Quarrel aſide, and be content to be mewed up in this Cloaths-preſs together, or ſtay where you are, and face it out————— there is no Help for it

Flo Put me any where, rather than that, come, come, let me in   [*He opens the Preſs, and ſhe goes in.*

Iſis I'll ſee her hang'd, befoie I'll go into the Place where ſhe is —I'll truſt Foitune with my Deliverance. Here uſ d to be a Pair of back Stairs, I'll try to find them out   [*Exit*

Enter Felix *and* Frederick.

Fel. Was you aſleep, Sirrah, that you did not hear me call ?

Liſs. I did hear you, and arſwer'd you, I was comirg, Sir.

Fel. Go, get the Horſes ready, I ll leave *Liſlon* to night never to ſee it more.

Liſs Hey day! what's the Matter now ?   [*Exit*

Frid. Pray tell me, *Don Felix* what has ruffled your Tempei thus ?

Fel A Woman—Oh Friend, who can name Woman, ard forget Inconſtancy !

Fred This from a Perſon of mean Education were excuſable ſuch low Suſpicions have their Source from vulgar Converſation, Men of your politer Taſte never raſhly cenſure ———— Come, this is ſome groundleſs Jea- louſy—Love raiſes many Fears

Fel. No, my Ears conveyed the Truth into my Heart, and Reaſon juſtifies my Anger *Volante's* falſe, and I have nothing left but tree, in *Liſbon*, which can make me wiſh ever to ſee it more, except Revenge up- on my Rival, of whom I am ignorant Oh, that ſome Miracle wou'd reveal him to me, that I might thro' his Heart puniſh thy Infidelity.

Enter Liſſardo.

Liſs Oh! Sir, here's your Father *Don Lopez* coming up

Fel Does he know that I am here ?

Liſs I can't tell, Sir, he aſk'd for *Don Frederick.*

Frid Did he ſee you ?

Liſs I believe not, Sir, for as ſoon as I ſaw him, I ran back to give my Maſtei notice   *Fel*

Fel Keep out of his Sight then——And, dear *Frederick*, permit me to retire into the next Room, for I know the old Gentleman will be very much difpleafed at my Return without his Leave.   [*Exit.*

Fred Quick, quick, begone, he is here

Enter Don Lopez, *fpeaking as he enters.*

Lop. Mr *Alguazile*, wait you without till I call for you. *Frederick*, an Affair brings me here — which—requires Privacy—So that if you have any Body within Ea.-fhot, pray order them to retire.

Fred. We are private, my Lord, fpeak freely.

Lop. Why then, Sir, I muft tell you, that you had better have pitch'd upon any Man in *Portugal* to have injur'd, than myfelf.

I l [*Peeping*] What means my Father?

Fred. I underftand you not, my Lord

Lop Tho' I am old, I have a Son——Alas! Why name I him? He knows not the Difhonour of my Houfe

Fel I am confounded! The Difhonour of his Houfe!

Fred Explain yourfelf, my Lord! I am not confcious of any difhonourable Action to any Man, much lefs to your Lordfhip

Lop 'Tis faife! you have debauch'd my Daughter.

Fel. Debauch'd my Sifter! Impoffible! He could not, durft not be that Villain.

Fred My Lord, I fcorn fo foul a Charge.

Lop. You have debauch'd her Duty at leaft, therefore inftantly reftore her to me, or by St *Anthony* I'll make you

Fred. Reftore her, my Lord! Where fhall I find her?

Lop. I have thofe that will fwear fhe is here in your Houfe

Fel. Ha! in this Houfe!

Fred You are mifinformed, my Lord, upon my Reputation I have not feen *Donna Ifabella*, fince the Abfence of *Don Felix.*

Lop Then pray, Sir——if I am not too inquifitive, what Motive had you for thofe Objections you made againft her Marriage with *Don Guzman* yefterday?

Fred The Difagreeablenefs of fuch a Match, I fear'd, wou'd give your Daughter Caufe to curfe her Duty, if fhe

B 5   *comply'd*

comply'd with your Demands; that was all, my Lord!

Lop. And so you help'd her thro' the Window to make her disobey.

Fel. Ha, my Sister gone! Oh Scandal to our Blood!

Fred This is insulting me, my Lord, when I assure you I have neither seen, nor know any Thing of your Daughter —— If she is gone, the Contrivance was her own, and you may thank your Rigour for it.

Lop. Very well, Sir; however my Rigour shall make bold to search your House Here, call in the *Alguazile*—

Flora [*Peeping*] The *Alguazile!* What in the Name of Wonder will become of me!

Fred. The *Alguazile!* My Lord, you'll repent this.

Enter Alguazile *and Attendants.*

Lop No, Sir, 'tis you that will repent it. I charge you, in the King's Name, to assist me in finding my Daughter —— Before you leave no Part of the House unsearch'd; come, follow me [*Gets towards the Door where* Felix *is,* Frederick *draws, and plants himself before the Door*

Fred Sir, I must first know by what Authority you pretend to search my House, before you enter here

Alg How! Sir, dare you presume to draw your Sword upon the Representative of Majesty? I am, Sir, I am his Majesty's *Alguazile*, and the very Quintessence of Authority —— therefore put up your Sword, or I shall order you to be knock'd down—— For know, Sir, the Breath of an *Alguazile* is as dangerous as the Breath of a *Demi-Culverin*

Lop She is certainly in that Room, by his guarding the Door —— if he disputes your Authority, knock him down, I say.

Col I shall show you some Sport first! The Woman you look for is not here, but there is something in this Room, which I'll preserve from your Sight at the Hazard of my Life

Lop Enter, I say, nothing but my Daughter can be there—force his Sword from him. [Felix *comes out and joins* Frederick.

Col What! Dare you assassinate a Man in his own House

Lop.

Lop. Oh, oh, oh, *Misericordia,* what do I see, my Son.

Alo. Ha, his Son! Here's five hundred Pounds good, my Brethren, if *Antonio* dies, and that's in the Surgeon's Power, and he's in love with my Daughter, you know — *Don Felix!* I command you to surrender yourself into the Hands of Justice, in order to raise me and my Posterity; and in Consideration you lose your Head to gain me five hundred Pounds, I'll have your Generosity recorded on your Tomb stone — at my own proper Cost and Charge—I hate to be ungrateful.

Fred Here's a generous Dog now————

Lop Oh that ever I was born——Hold, hold, hold

Fred Did I not tell you, you wou'd repent, my Lord? What ho! Within there [*Enter Servants*] arm your selves, and let not a Man in nor out but *Felix*——— Look ye, *Alguzile,* when you would betray my Friend for filthy Lucre, I shall no more regard you as an Officer of Justice, but as a Thief and Robber thus resist you.

Fel. Generous *Frederick!* Come on, Sir, we'll show you Play for the five hundred Pounds.

Alg. Fall on, seize the Money right or wrong, ye Rogues   [*They fight.*

Lop Hold, hold, *Alguzile;* I'll give you the five hundred Pounds; that is, my Bond to pay upon *Antonio's* Death, and twenty Pistoles however things go, for you and these honest Fellows to drink my Health.

Alg. Say you so, my Lord! Why look ye my Lord, I bear the young Gentleman no ill-will, my Lord, if I get but the five hundred Pounds, my Lord——— why, look ye, my Lord———'Tis the same Thing to me whether your Son be hang'd or not, my Lord.

Fel Scoundrels.——— ———

Lop. Ay, well thou art a good-natur'd Fellow, that is the Truth on't ——— Come then we'll to the Tavern, and sign and seal this Minute. O *Felix,* be careful of thyself, or thou wilt break my Heart   [*Exit Lopez,* Alguzile *and Attendants.*

Fel Now, *Frederick,* though I ought to thank you for your Care of me, yet till I am satisfied as to my Father's Accusation, I can't return the Acknowledgments I owe you. Know you aught relating to my Sister?

Fred. I hope my Faith and Truth are known to you——

And

...rd here by both I swear, I am ignorant of every Thing relating to your Father's Charge

Fel Enough, I do believe thee.   Oh Fortune! where will thy Malice end!

Ser Sir, I bring you joyful News, I am told that D...... is out of Danger, and now in the Palace.

Fel I wish it be true, then I'm at Liberty to watch my Rival, and pursue my Sister.   Prithee, *Frederick*, in... form thyself of the Truth of this Report.

Fred I will this Minute —Do you hear, let no body into *Don Felix* till my Return   [*Exit.*

Ser I'll observe, Sir.   [*Exit*

Flo. (*Peeping*) They have almost frighted me out of my Wits——I'm sure ——— Now *Felix* is alone, I have a good Mind to pretend I came with a Message from my Lady, but then how shall I say I came into the Cupboard?   [*Aside.*

Enter a Servant, seeming to oppose the Entrance of some body.

Ser. I tell you, Madam, *Don Felix* is not here.

Vio (*Within*) I tell you, Sir, he is here, and I will see him (*breaks in*) You are as difficult of Access, Sir, as first Minister of State

Felo My Stars! My Lady here! [*Shuts the Press close.*

If your Visit was design'd to *Frederick*, Madam, he's abroad

Vio. No, Sir, the Visit is to you.

Fel You are very punctual in your Ceremonies, Madam

Vio Tho' I did not come to return your Visit, but to take that which your Civility ought to have brought me.

Fel If my Ears, my Eyes and my Understanding ly'd, then I am in your Debt, else not, Madam.

Vio. I will not charge them with a Term so gross, to say they ly'd, but call it a Mistake, nay call it any thing to excuse my *Felix*—Cou'd I, think ye, cou'd I put off my Pride so far, poorly to dissemble a Passion which I did not feel? Or seek a Reconciliation, with what I did not love? Do but consider, if I had entertain'd another, shou'd not I rather embrace this Quarrel pleas'd with the Occasion that rid me of your Visits,

                                                                and

and gave me Freedom to enjoy the Choice which you
think I have made; have I any Interest in thee but my
Love? Or am I bound by ought but Inclination to sub-
mit and follow thee——No Law whilst single binds us to
obey, but you by Nature, and Education, are oblig'd
to pay a deference to all Woman-kind

Fel These are fruitless Arguments · 'Tis most certain thou wert dearer to these Eyes than all that Heaven
e'er gave to charm the Sense of Man, but I wou'd rather
tear them out, than suffer them to delude my Reason,
and enslave my Peace.

Vio Can you love without Esteem? And where is
the Esteem for her you still suspect? Oh, *Felix!* There
is a Delicacy——in Love, which equals even a religious
Faith! true Love ne'er doubts the Object it adores, and
Sceptics there will disbelieve their Sight

Enter Servant.

Fel Your Notions are too refin'd for mine, Madam.
How now, what do you want?

Ser Only my Master's Cloak out of this Press, Sir,
that's all ————Oh! the Devil, the Devil

[*Opens the Press, sees* Flora, *and roars out.*

Vio. Ha, a Woman conceal'd! Very well, *Felix!*

Flo. Discover'd! Nay then Legs befriend me.

[*Runs out.*

Fel A Woman in the Press!   [*Enter* Lissardo.
How the Devil came a Woman there, Sirrah?

Liss. What shall I say now?

Vio Now *Lissardo,* shew your Wit to bring your
Master off

Liss. Off, Madam! Nay, nay, nay, there, there needs
no great Wit to, to, to bring him off, Madam, for she
did, and she did not come as, as, as, as, a, a, a Man may
say directly to, to, to, to, speak with my Master, Madam.

Vio I see by your Stammering, *Lissardo,* that your
Invention is at a very low Ebb.

Fel. 'Sdeath, Rascal! speak without Hesitation, and
the Truth too, or I shall stick my Stilletto in your Guts.

Vio No, no, your Master mistakes, he wou'd not have
you speak the Truth

Fel Madam, my Sincerity wants no Excuse

Liss. I am so confounded between one and the other,
that I can't think of a Lye.   [*Aside.*

Fel. Sirrah, fetch me this Woman back inftantly, I'll know what Bufinefs fhe had here!

Vio. Not a Step, your Mafter fhan't be put to the Blufh.—Come, a Truce, *Felix!* Do you afk me no more Queftions about the Window, and I'll forgive this.

Fel. I fcorn Forgivenefs where I own no Crime, but your Soul, confcious of its Guilt, wou'd fain lay hold of this Occafion to blend your Treafon with my Innocence.

Vio Infolent! Nay, if inftead of owning your Fault you endeavour to infult my Patience, I muft tell you, Sir, you don't behave yourfelf like that Man of Honour you wou'd be taken for; you ground your Quarrel with me upon your own Inconftancy; 'tis plain you are falfe yourfelf, and wou'd make me the Aggreffor——It was not for nothing the Fellow oppos'd my Entrance ——This laft Ufage has given me back my Liberty, and now my Father's Will fhall be obeyed without the leaft Reluctance   [*Exit.*

Fel Oh, ftubborn, ftubborn Heart, what wilt thou do? Her Father's Will fhall be obeyed, Ha! That carries her to a Cloyfter, and cuts off all my Hopes at once——By Heaven fhe fhall not, muft not leave me! No, fhe is not falfe, at leaft my Love now reprefents her true, becaufe I fear to lofe her· Ha! Villain, art thou here [*turns upon Liffardo*] tell me this Moment who this Woman was, and for what Intent fhe was here conceal'd ————Or

Liff Ay, good Sir, forgive me, and I'll tell you the whole Truth.   [*falls on his Knees.*

Fel Out with it ther————

Liff. It, it, it, was Mis *Flora*, Sir, *Donna Violante's* Woman—vou muft know, Sir, we have had a fneaking Kindnefs for one another a great while—She was not willing you fhould know it, fo when fhe heard your Voice fhe ran into the Cloaths-Prefs, I wou'd have told you this at firft, but I was afraid of her Lady's knowing it, this is the Truth as I hope for a whole Skin, Sir.

Fel If it be not, I'll not leave you a whole Bone in it, Sirrah————fly, and obferve if *Violante* goes directly home

Liff Yes, Sir, yes.   [*Exit.*
                                                 Fel.

Fel. I muſt convince her of my Faith: Oh! how irreſolute is a Lover's Heart! My Reſentments cool'd when her's grew high——Nor can I ſtruggle longer with my Fate; I cannot quit her, no I cannot, ſo abſolute a Conqueſt has ſhe gain'd——Woman's the greateſt ſovereign Power on Earth.

> *In vain Men ſtrive their Tyranny to quit,*
> *Their Eyes command and force us to ſubmit.*
> *So have I ſeen a mettled Courſer fly,*
> *Tear up the Ground, and toſs his Rider high,*
> *Till ſome experienc'd Maſter found the Way,*
> *With Spur and Rein to make his Pride obey*

SCENE *the Terriero de Paſſa.*

Enter Colonel *and* Iſabella *veil'd.* Gibby *at a Diſtance*

Col Then you ſay, it is impoſſible for me to wait of you home, Madam.

Iſab. I ſay it is inconſiſtent with my Circumſtances, Colonel, and that Way impoſſible for me to admit of it.

Col Conſent to go with me then——I lodge at one *Don Frederick's*, a Merchant juſt by here, he is a very honeſt Fellow, and I dare confide in his Secreſy.

Iſab Ha, does he lodge there? Pray Heaven I am not diſcover'd. [*Aſide.*

Col What ſay you, my Charmer? ſhall we breakfaſt together? I have ſome of the beſt Bohea in the Univerſe.

Iſ. Puh! Bohea! is that the beſt Treat you can give a Lady at your Lodgings————Colonel!

Col Well hinted————No, no, no, I have other Things at thy Service, Child

Iſab. What are thoſe Things, pray?

Col My Heart, Soul, and Body into the Bargain

Iſab Has the laſt no Incumbrance upon it, can you make a clear Title, Colonel?

Col. All Freehold, Child, and I'll afford thee a very good Bargain. [*embraces her.*

Gib. Au my Sol, they mak muckle Wards about it, Ife ſeer weary with ſtanding, Ife e'en tak a Sleep. [*Lies down*

Iſab If I take a Leaſe it muſt be for Life, Colonel.

Col Thou ſhalt have me as long, or as little Time as thou

thou

thou wilt; my Dear, come, let's to my Lodging, and we'll sign and seal this Minute

Isab Oh, not so fast, Colonel, there are many Things to be adjusted before the Lawyer and the Parson comes.

Col. The Lawyer and Parson! No, no, ye little Rogue, we can finish our Affairs without the Help of the Law——or the Gospel

Isab. Indeed but we can't, Colonel

Col. Indeed! Why, hast thou then trapann'd me out of my warm Bed this Morning for nothing! Why, this is shewing a Man half famish'd a well-furnish'd Larder, then clapping a Padlock on the Door, till you starve him quite.

Isab If you can find in your Heart to say Grace, Colonel, you shall keep the Key.

Col. I love to see my Meat before I give Thanks, Madam, therefore uncover thy Face, Child and I'll tell thee more of my Mind——if I like you ————

Isab. I dare not risk my Reputation upon your If's, Colonel, and so adieu   [*Going.*

Col. Nay, nay, nay, we must not part.

Isab As you ever hope to see me more, suspend your Curiosity now, one Step farther loses me for ever ——— Show yourself a Man of Honour, and you shall find me a Woman of Honour.   [*Exit.*

Col Well, for once I'll trust to a blind Bargain, Madam——[*Kisses her Hand and parts*] But I shall be too cunning for your Ladyship if *Gibby* observes my Orders Methinks these Intrigues, which relate to the Mind, are very insipid——The Conversation of Bodies is much more diverting——Ha! What do I see, my Rascal asleep? Sirrah, did not I charge you to watch the Lady? And is it thus you observe my Orders, ye Dog? [*Kicks him all this while, and he shrugs, and rubs his Eyes, and yawns.*

Gib. That's treu, an I k yer Honour; but I thought that when ence ye had her in yer awn Honds, yee mit a ordered her yer sal weel eneugh without me, en ye ken, an lik yer Honour.

Col Sirrah hold your impertinent Tongue, and make haste after her if you don't bring me some Account of her, never dare to see my Face again   [*Exit.*

Gib. Ay! This is bony Wark indeed, to run three
                                                        hundred

nundred Mile to this wicked Town, and before I can
well fill my Weem, to be fent a Whore-hunting after
this black fhee Devil—What Gat fal I gang to fpeer
for this Wutch now ? Ah, for a ruling Elder——or the
Kirk's Treafurer——or his Mon——I'd gar my Mafter
mak twa of this ; —— But I am feer there's na fike
honeft People here, or there wou'd na be fo muckle
Sculdudrie*

(*Enter an* Englifh *Soldier paffing along*)

Gib Geud Mon, did ye fee a Woman, a Lady, ony
gate here away enow ?

Eng Man, Yes, a great many   What kind of a
Woman is it you enquire after ?

Gib Geud troth, fhe's ne Kenfpekle, fhe's aw in a
Cloud.——

Eng. Man What ! 'tis fome High-land Monfter which
you brought over with you, I fuppofe, I fee no fuch,
not I, Kenfpekle, quotha !

Gib. Huly, huly, Mon, the Deel pike out yer Eyn, and
then you'll fee the bater, ye *Englifh* Bag Pudin Tike

Eng. Man. What fays the Fellow ? [*Turning to* Gibby.

Gib. Say ! I fay I am a better Fellow than e'er ftude
upon yer Shanks——an gin I heer meer a yer Din,
Deel a my Saul, Sir, but Ife crack yer Crown

Eng Man. Get you gone, you *Scotch* Rafcal, and
thank your Heathen Dialect, which I don't underftand,
that you han't your Bones broke.

Gib. Ay ! an ye de no underftond a *Scots* Man's
Tongue ——Ife fee gin ye can underftond a *Scots* Man's
Gripe. Wha's the better Mon now, Sir ?   [*Lays hold of*
him, *ftriles up his Heels, and gets aftride over him.*
Here Violante *croffes the Stage* , Gibby *jumps up from the*
Man, *and brufhes up to* Violante.

Gib I vow, Madam, but I am glad that yee and I
are foregather'd

Vio What wou'd the Fellow have ?

Gib Nothing, away, Madam, wo worthy yer Heart,
what a muckle deel a Mifchief had you like to bring
upon poor *Gibby* ?

Vio. The Man's drunk——

Gib. In troth am I not——An gin I had not fond
                                                              ye,

* Fornication.

ye, Madam, the Laird knows when I fhould ; for my Mafter bat me nere gang Heam, without Tydings of yee, Madam.

Vio. Sirrah, get about your Bufinefs, or I'll have your Bones drubb'd.

Gib. Geud Faith, my Mafter has e'en dun that te yer Honds, Madam.

Vio. Who is your Mafter, Friend ?

Gib Mony e'en fpiers the gat they ken right weel ——It is no fo lang fen ye parted wi him, I wifh he ken yee hafe as weel as ye ken him.

Vio. Pugh, the Creature's mad or miftakes me for fome Body elfe ; and I fhou'd be as mad as he, to talk to him any longer.

Enter Liffardo *at the upper End of the Stage.*

Liff. So, fhe's gone home, I fee. What did that *Scotch* Fellow want with her ? I'll try to find it out ; perhaps I may difcover fomething that may make my Mafter Friends with me again.

Gib. Are you gaune, Madam, a Deel fcope in yer Company ; for I'm as weefe as I was ? but I'll bide and fee whafe Houfe it is, gin I can meet with ony civil Body to fpier at.————Weel of aw Men in the Warld, I think our *Scots* Men the greateft Feuls, to leave their weel favour'd honeft Women at Heam, to rin walloping after a Pack of Gycarlings here, that fhame to fhew their Faces, and peer Men like me, are forc'd to be their Pimps ! a Pimp ! Godfwarbit, *Gibby*'s ne'er be a Pimp ——An yet in troth it is a threving Trade ; I remember a Countryman aw mi aen, that by ganging a fikle like Errants as I am now, came to gat Preferment: My Lad, wot yee wha lives here ?   [*Turns and fees* Liffardo.

Liff Don Pedro de Mendofa.

Gib. And did you fee a Lady gang in but now ?

Liff Yes, I did.

Gib. And dee ken her tee ?

Liff It was *Donna Violante* his Daughter ; what the Devil makes him fo inquifitive ? Here is fomething in it, that's certain. 'Tis a cold Morning, Brother, what think you of a Dram ?

Gib. In troth, very weel, Sir.

Liff. You feem an honeft Fellow , prithee let's drink to our better Acquaintance.   *Gib.*

Gib. Wi aw my Heart, Sir, gang your gat to the next House, and Ise follow ye

   Liss. Come along then.   [*Exit.*

   Gib *Don Pedro de Mendosa*————*Donna Violante* his Daughter; that's as right as my Leg now ——— Ise need na meer, I'll tak a Drink, an then to my Master.————

   Ise bring him News will mak his Heart full Blee ;
   Gin he rewards it not, Deel pimp for me.   [Exit.

ACT IV.

SCENE, Violante's *Lodgings.*

Enter Isabella *in a gay Temper, and* Violante *out of Humour.*

Isab. MY Dear, I have been seeking you this half Hour to tell you the most lucky Adventure.

Vio. And you have pitched upon the most unlucky Hour for it, that you could possibly have found in the whole Four and Twenty.

Isab. Hang unlucky Hours, I won't think of them; I hope all my Misfortunes are past.

Vio And mine all to come.

Isab. I have seen the Man I like.

Vio. And I have seen the Man that I cou'd wish to hate.

Isab, And you must assist me in discovering whether he can like me or not.

Vio You have assisted me in such a Discovery already, I thank ye.

Isab. What say you, my Dear?

Vio. I say I am very unlucky at Discoveries, *Isabella*; I have too lately made one pernicious to my Ease, your Brother is false.

Isab. Impossible !

Vio Most true

Isab. Some Villain has traduc'd him to you.

Vio No, *Isabella*, I love too well to trust the Eyes of others; I never credit the ill-judging World, or form Suspicions upon vulgar Censures; no, I had ocular Proof of his Ingratitude.

Isab. Then am I most unhappy; my Brother was the only Pledge of Faith betwixt us; if he has forfeited
                            your

your Favour, I have no Title to your Friendship.

Vio You wrong my Friendship, *Isabella*, your own Merit entitles you to every thing within my *Power*.

Isab. Generous Maid —— But may I not know what Grounds you have to think my Brother false.

Vio. Another time —— But tell me, *Isabella*, how can I serve you?

Isab Thus then —— The Gentleman that brought me hither, I have seen and talk'd with upon the *Terrero de Passa* this Morning, and I find him a Man of Sense, Generosity, and good Humour, in short, he is every Thing that I could like for a Husband, and I have dispatch'd Mrs. *Flora* to bring him hither; I hope you'll forgive the Liberty I have taken

Vio Hither, to what Purpose?

Isab. To the great universal Purpose, Matrimony.

Vio. Matrimony! Why, do you design to ask him?

Isab No, *Violante*, you must do that for me.

Vio I thank you for the Favour you design me, but desire to be excus'd I manage my own Affairs too ill, to be trusted with those of other People, besides, if my Father should find a Stranger here, it might make him hurry me into a *Monastry* immediately; I can't for my Life admire your Conduct, to encourage a Person altogether unknown to you. —— 'Twas very imprudent to meet him this Morning, but much more so to send for him hither, knowing what Inconveniency you have already drawn upon me

Isab I am not insensible, how far my Misfortunes have embarras'd you; and, if you please, sacrifice my Quiet to your own

Vio. Unkindly urg'd —— Have I not preferr'd your Happiness to every thing that's dear to me?

Isab. I know thou hast——Then do not deny me this last Request, when a few Hours, perhaps, may render my Condition able to clear thy Fame, and bring my Brother to thy Feet for Pardon.

Vio. I wish you don't repent of this Intrigue. I suppose he knows you are the same Woman that he brought in here last Night.

Isab. Not a Syllable of that; I met him veil'd, and to prevent his knowing the House, I order'd Mrs. *Flora*

to bring him by the back Door into the Garden.

Vio The very Way which *Felix* comes, if they should meet, there would be fine Work — Indeed, my Dear, I can't approve of your Design.

Enter Flora.

Flor Madam, the Colonel waits your Pleasure.

Vio. How durst you go upon such a Message, Mistress, without acquainting me?

Isab 'Tis too late to dispute that now, dear *Violante,* I acknowledge the Rashness of the Action —— But consider the Necessity of my Deliverance

Vio That indeed is a weighty Consideration; well, what am I to do?

Isab In the next Room I'll give you Instructions! in the mean time, Mrs. *Flora,* show the Colonel into this. [*Exit* Flora *one Way,* and Isabella *and* Violante *another.*

Re-enter Flora *with the* Colonel.

Flo The Lady will wait on you presently, Sir [*Exit.*

Col Very well—This is a very fruitful Soil. I have not been here quite four and Twenty Hours, and I have three Intrigues upon my Hands already, but I hate the Chase, without partaking of the Game. [*Enter* Violante *veil'd*] Ha, a fine siz'd Woman —— Pray Heaven she proves handsome —— I am come to obey your Ladyship's Commands

Vio Are you sure of that Colonel?

Col If you be not very unreasonable indeed, Madam; A Man is but a Man. [*Takes her Hand and kisses it.*

Vio Nay, we have no Time for Compliments, Colonel.

Col I understand you, Madam —— *Montre moy votre Chambre* [*Takes her in his Arms.*

Vio Nay, nay, hold Colonel, my Bed chamber is not to be enter'd without a certain Purchase

Col Purchase! Humph, this is some kept Mistress, I suppose, who industriously lets out her leisure Hours. [*Aside*] Look ye, Madam, you must consider we Soldiers are not over-stock'd with Money — But we make ample Satisfaction in Love; we have a World of Courage upon our Hands now, you know — Then prithee use a Conscience, and I'll try if my Pocket can come up to your Price [*Puts his Hand into his Pocket.*

Vio Nay, don't give yourself the Trouble of drawing

, our

your Purse, Colonel, my Design is levell'd at your Person, if that be at your own Disposal.

Col. Ah, that it is Faith, Madam, and I'll settle it as firmly upon thee ———

Vio As Law can do it.

Col Hang Law in Love-affairs; thou shalt have Right and Title to it out of pure Inclination ———A matrimonial Hint again! Gad, I fancy the Women have a Project on Foot to transplant the Union into *Portugal.*

Vio Then you have an Aversion to Matrimony, Colonel; did you never see a Woman, in all your Travels, that you cou'd like for a Wife?

Col. A very odd Question——Do you really expect that I should speak Truth now?

Vio. I do, if you expect to be dealt with, Colonel.

Col. Why then———Yes.

Vio. Is she in your Country, or this?

Col. This is a very pretty Kind of a Catechism but I don't conceive which Way it turns to Edification. In this Town, I believe, Madam.

Vio. Her Name is ———

Col. Ay, how is she call'd, Madam?

Vio Nay, I ask you that, Sir.

Col. Oh, Oh, why she is call'd——Pray, Madam, how is it you spell your Name?

Vio. Oh, Colonel, I am not the happy Woman, nor do I wish it.

Col. No, I'm sorry for that.——What the Devil does she mean by all these Questions?   [*Aside*

Vio. Come, Colonel, for once be sincere.——Perhaps you may not repent it.

Col. Faith, Madam, I have an Inclination to Sincerity, but I'm afraid you'll call my Manners in Question This is like to be but a silly Adventure, here's so much Sincerity required.   [*Aside*

Vio. Not at all. I prefer Truth before Compliment, in this Affair.

Col Why then to be plain with you, Madam, a Lady last Night wounded my Heart by a Fall from a Window, whose Person I cou'd be content to take, as my Father took my Mother, till Death do us part. ———
But whom she is, or how distinguished, whether Maid,
Wife,

Wife, or Widow, I can't inform you; perhaps you are she.

Vio. Not to keep you in Sufpence, I am not she, but I can give you an Account of her. That Lady is a Maid of Condition, has ten thoufand Pounds; and if you are a fingle Man, her Perfon and Fortune are at your Service.

Col I accept the Offer with the highest Tranfports; but fay, my charming Angel, art thou not she? *(offers to embrace her)* This is a lucky Adventure.   [*Afide.*

Vio Once again, Colonel, I tell you I am not she—— But at Six this Evening you shall find her on the *Ter-riero de Paffa*, with a white Handkerchief in her Hand; get a Priest ready, and you know the reft.

Col. I shall infallibly obferve your Directions, Madam.

Enter Flora *haftily, and whifpers* Violante, *who ftarts and feems furprifed.*

Vio Ha, *Felix* croffing the Garden, fay you, what shall I do now?

Col You feem furpriz'd, Madam.

Vio. Oh, Colonel, my Father is coming hither, and if he finds you here, I am ruin'd!

Col. Odflife, Madam, thruft me any where; can't I go out this Way?

Vio. No, no, no, he comes that Way. how shall I prevent their Meeting? Here, here, ftep into my Bedchamber, and be ftill, as you value her you love, don't ftir till you've Notice, as ever you hope to have her in your Arms

Col. On that Condition, I'll not breathe.   [*Exit.*

        Enter Felix.

Fel I wonder where this Dog of a Servant is all this while——But she is at home I find——How coldly she regards me.——You look, *Violante*, as if the Sight of me were troublefome to you.

Vio Can I do otherwife, when you have the Affurance to approach me, after what I faw to-day!

Fel. Affurance, rather call it good Nature, after what I heard laft Night; but such regard to Honour, have I in my Love to you, I cannot bear to be fufpected, nor fuffer you to entertain falfe Notions of my Truth, without endeavouring to convince you of my Innocence, fo

                     2   much

much good Nature have I more than you, *Violante*,
———— Pray give me Leave to afk your Woman one
Queftion , my Man affures me fhe was the Perfon you
faw at my Lodgings.

Flo. I confefs it, Madam, and afk your Pardon.

Vio Impudent Baggage, not to undeceive me fooner;
what Bufinefs cou'd you have there ?

Fel. Liffardo and fhe, it feems, imitate you and I.

Flo I love to follow the Example of my Betters,
Madam.

Fel. I hope I am juftified ————

Vio. Since we are to paft, *Felix*, there needs no Juf-
tification.

Fel Methinks you talk of parting as a Thing indifferent to you , can you forget how I have lov'd ?

Vio I wifh I could forget my own Paffion , I fhou'd
with lefs concern remember yours ———— But for Mrs.
Flora ————

Fel. You muft forgive her ; ———— Muft, did I fay ? I
fear I have no Power to impofe, tho' the Injury was
done to me.

Vio 'Tis harder to pardon an Injury done to what we
love than to ourfelves, but at your Requeft, *Felix*, I do
forgive her , go watch my Father, *Flora*, left he fhould
awake and furprize us.

Flo. Yes, Madam. [*Exit* Flora.

Fel Doft thou then love me, *Violante* ?

Vio What need of Repetition from my Tongue,
when every Look confeffes what you afk ?

Fel. Oh ! let no Man judge of Love but thofe who
feel it ; what wonderous Magic lies in one kind Look !
———— One tender Word deftroys a Lover's Rage, and
melts his fierceft Paffion into foft Complaint. Oh the
Window, *Violante,* would ft thou but clear that one
Sufpicion !

Vio Prithee, no more of that, my *Felix*, a little Time
fhall bring thee perfect Satisfaction

Fel Well, *Violante*, on that Condition you think no
more of a Monaftry————I'll wait with Patience for
this mighty Secret

Vio Ah, *Felix*, Love generally gets the better of Religion in us Women Refolutions made in the Heat of
Paffion, ever diffolve upon Reconciliation. *Exit*

Enter Flora *haftily.*

Flo. Oh, Madam, Madam, Madam! my Lord your Father has been in the Garden, and lock'd the back Door, and comes muttering to himfelf this Way

Vio. Then we are caught. Now, *Felix,* we are undone

Fel. Heavens forbid, this is moft unlucky! let me ftep into your Bed chamber, he won't look under the Bed, there I may conceal myfelf. [*runs to the Door, and pufhes it open a little.*

Vio. My Stars! if he goes in there he'll find the Colonel————No, no, *Felix,* that's no fafe Place, my Father often goes thither; and fhould you cough, or fneeze, we are loft.

Fel. Either my Eye deceiv'd me, or I faw a Man within; I'll watch him clofe————fhe fha'll deal with the Devil, if fhe conveys him out without my Knowledge. [*Afide*] What fhall I do then?

Vio. Blefs me how I tremble!

Flo. Oh, Invention, Invention!—I have it, Madam; here, here, here, Sir, off with your Sword, and I'll fetch you a Difguife. (*Runs in and fetches out a Riding Hood.*)

Fel. Ay, ay, any thing to avoid *Don Pedro.*

Vio. Oh! quick, quick, quick, I fhall die with Apprehenfion. (Flo. *a puts the Riding-Hood on* Felix.

Flo. Be fure you don't fpeak a Word!

Fel. Not for the *Indies* ————But I fhall obferve you clofer than you imagine. [*Afide.*

Pedro. [*within*] *Violante* where are you, Child? [*Enter* Don Pedro] Why, how came the Garden-Door open? Ha! How now, who have we here?

Vio. Humph, he'll certainly difcover him. [*Afide.*

Flo. 'Tis my Mother, and pleafe you, Sir [*She and* Felix *both court*

Pedro. Your Mother! By St *Anthony,* fhe's a Strapper, why, you are a Dwarf to her————How many Children have you, good Woman?

Vio. Oh! if he fpeaks we are loft [*Afide.*

Flo. Oh! Dear *Senior,* fhe cannot hear you, fhe has been deaf thefe twenty Years

Pedro. Alas, poor Woman ——— Why, you muffle her up as if fhe were blind too

C   *Fe.*

Fel Would I were fairly off.   [*Aside.*

Pedro Turn up her Hood.

Vio Undone for ever—St. *Anthony* forbid : Oh, Sir, she has the dreadfullest unlucky Eyes ————Pray don't look upon them ; I made her keep her Hood shut on Purpose.————Oh, oh, oh, oh !

Pedro Eyes ! Why, what's the Matter with her Eyes ?

Flo My poor Mother, Sir, is much afflicted with the Cholick, and about two Months ago she had it grievously in her Stomach, and was over-persuaded to take a Dram of filthy *English Geneva*--Which immediately flew up into her Head, and caused such a Defluxion in her Eyes, that she could never since bear the Day-light

Pedro Say you so ?—Poor Woman !— Well, make her sit down, *Violante*, and give her a Glass of Wine

Vio. Let her Daughter give her a Glass below, Sir; for my Part, she has frighted me so, I shan't be my self these two Hours.   I am sure her Eyes are evil Eyes.

Fel Well hinted

Pedro Well, well, do so   Evil Eyes, there is no evil Eyes, Child.   [*Exit* Felix *and* Flora.

Vio I'm glad he's gone.

Pedro Hast thou heard the News, *Violante* ?

Vio What News, Sir ?

Pedro Why, *Vasquez* tells me, that *Don Lopez*'s Daughter *Isabella* is run away from her Father, that Lord has very ill Fortune with his Children---Well, I'm glad my Daughter has no Inclination to Mankind, that my House is plagu'd with no Suitors.   [*Aside*

Vio. This is the first Word ever I heard of it ; I pity her Frailty ——

Pedro. Well said, *Violante*.—— Next Week I intend thy Happiness shall begin.   [*Enter* Flora

Vio. I don't intend to stay so long, I thank you, Papa   [*Aside.*

Pedro My Lady *Abbess* writes Word she longs to see thee, and has provided every Thing in Order for thy Reception —Thou wilt lead a happy Life, my Girl— Fifty Times before that of Matrimony, where an extravagant Coxcomb might make a Beggar of thee, or an ill-natur'd surly Dog break thy Heart.

Flo. Break thy Heart ! She had as good have her
Bones

Bones broke as to be a Nun ; I am fure I had, rather of the two.——You are wonderous kind, Sir, but if I had fuch a Father, I know what I wou'd do

Pedro Why, what wou'd you do, Minx, ha ?

Flo I wou'd tell him I had as good a Right and Title to the Law of Nature, and the End of the Crea-tion, as he had——— ——

Pedro You wou'd, Miftrefs ; who the Devil doubts it ? A good Affurance is a Chamber-maid's Coat of Arms ' and Lying, and Contriving, the Supporters. —— Your Inclinations are on tip-toe, it feems--If I were your Father, Houfewife, I'd have a Pennance enjoin'd you, fo ftrict, that you fhould not be able to turn you in your Bed for a Month——You are enough to fpoil your Lady, Houfewife, if fhe had not Abundance of Devotion.

Vio Fye, *Flora*, are you not afhamed to talk thus to my Father ? You faid yefterday you would be glad to go with me into the Monaftry.

Pedro. She go with thee! No, no, fhe's enough to debauch the whole Convent —— Well, Child, remem-ber what I faid to thee   Next Week——

Vio Ay, and what I am to do this too —— [*Afide.* I am all Obedient, Sir, I care not how foon I change my Condition

Flo But little does he think what Change fhe means.
[*Afide.*

Pedro Well faid, *Violante* ——— I am glad to find her fo willing to leave the World, but it is wholly ow-ing to my prudent Management, did fhe know that fhe might command her Fortune when fhe came at Age, or upon Day of Marriage, perhaps fhe'd change her Note. —— But I have always told her that her Grandfather left it with this Provifo, That fhe turn'd Nun now a fmall Part of this twenty thoufand Pounds provides for her in the Nunnery, and the reft is my own, there is nothing to be got in this Life without Policy [*Afide*] Well Child, I am going into the Country for two or three Days, to fettle fome Affairs with thy Uncle — And then——Come, help me on with my Cloak, Child.

Vio. Yes, Sir   [*Exit* Pedro *and* Violante.

Flo So, now for the Colonel. [*Goes to the Chamber-Door*] Hift, hift, Colonel.   [*Colonel peeping.*

Col.

Col. Is the Coaſt clear ?

Flo Yes, if you can climb , for you muſt get over the Waſh-houſe, and jump from the Garden-Wall into the Street

Col Nay, nay, I don't mind my Neck if my Incognita anſwers but thy Lady's Promiſe

　　　　　　　　　　　[*Exit* Colonel *and* Flora.

　　　　　Re-enter Pedro *and* Violante

Ped Good-bye, *Violant* , take care of thyſelf, Child.

Vio I wiſh you a good Journey, Sir—Now to ſet my Priſoner at Liberty　　　[*Enter* Felix *behind* Violante.

Fel I have lain perdue under the Stairs, till I watch'd the old Man out

Vio Sir, Sir, you may appear　　　[*Goes to the Door.*

Fel. May he ſo, Madam ?—I had Cauſe for my Suſpicion, I find, treacherous Woman.

Vio. Ha, *Felix* here ! Nay, then, all's diſcover'd.

Fel [*Draws*] Villain, whoe'er thou art, come out I charge thee, and take the Reward of thy adulterous Errand.

Vio. What ſhall I ſay ?—— Nothing but the Secret which I have ſworn to keep can reconcile this Quarrel

　　　　　　　　　　　[*Aſide.*

Fel A Coward ! Nay, then I'll fetch you out, think not to hide thyſelf ; no, by St. *Anthony*, an Altar ſhould not protect thee, even there I'd reach thy Heart, tho' all the Saints were arm'd in thy Defence.　　[*Exit.*

Vio. Defend me, Heaven ! What ſhall I do ? I muſt diſcover *Iſabella*, or here will be Murder.——

　　　　　Enter Flora.

Flo I have help'd the Colonel off clear, Madam

Vio. Say'ſt thou ſo, my Girl ? then I am arm'd.

　　　　　Re-enter Felix.

Fel. Where has the Devil in Compliance to your Sex convey'd him from my juſt Reſentment ?

Vio. Him, who do you mean, my dear inquiſitive Spark ? Ha, ha, ha, ha, you will never leave theſe jealous Whims ?

Fel Will you never ceaſe to impoſe upon me ?

Vio. You impoſe upon yourſelf, my Dear ; do you think I did not ſee you ? Yes, I did, and reſolved to put this Trick upon you , I knew, you'd take the Hint, and

　　　　　　　　　　　　　　　'ſoon

foon relapfe into your wonted Error How eafily your Jealoufy is fired ? I fhall have a bleffed Life with you.

Fel Was there nothing in it then, but only to try me ?

Vio Won't you believe your Eyes ?

Fel No, becaufe I find they have deceiv'd me ; well, I am convinc'd that faith is a neceffary in Love as in Religion ; for the Moment a Man lets a Woman know her Conqueft, he refigns his Senfes, and fees nothing but what fhe'd have him.

Vio And as foon as that Man finds his Love return'd, fhe becomes as errant a Slave, as if fhe had already faid after the Prieft

Fel The Prieft, *Violante*, would diffipate thofe Fears which caufe thefe Quarrels, when wilt thou make me happy ?

Vio To-morrow, I will tell thee . my Father is gone for two or three Days to my Uncle's we have Time enough to form our Affairs —But prithy leave me now, for I expect fome Ladies to vifit me.

Fel If you command it.—Fly fwift, ye Hours, and bring to-morrow on.——You defire I wou'd leave you, *Violante*.

Vio. I do at prefent.

Fel. *So much you reign the Sovereign of my Soul,*
    That I obey without the leaft Controul.   [Exit.

Enter Ifabella.

Ifab I am glad my Brother and you are reconcil'd, my Dear, and the Colonel efcap'd without his Knowledge , I was frighted out of my Wits when I heard him return —I know not how to exprefs my Thanks, Woman—for what you fuffer'd for my Sake, my grateful Acknowledgment fhall ever wait you , and to the World proclaim the Faith, Truth, and Honour of a Woman —

Vio Prithy don't compliment thy Friend, *Ifabella* — You heard the Colonel, I fuppofe

Ifab Every Syllable, and am pleas'd to find I do not love in vain

Vio. Thou haft caught his Heart, it feems; and an Hour hence may fecure his Perfon —Thou haft made hafty work on't Girl.

Ifab.

Isab. From thence I draw my Happiness, we shall have no Accounts to make up after Consummation.

She who for Years, protects her Lover's Pain,
And makes him wish, and wait, and sigh in vain,
To be his Wife, when late she gives Consent,
Finds half his Passion was in Courtship spent ;
Whilst they who boldly all Delays remove,
Find every Hour a fresh Supply of Love

ACT V.

Scene, Frederick's *House.*

Enter Felix *and* Frederick.

Fel THIS Hour has been propitious, I am reconcil'd to *Violante,* and you assure me *Antonio* is out of Danger.

Fred. Your Satisfaction is doubly mine.

Enter Liffardo.

Fel What Haste you made, Sirrah, to bring me Word if *Violante* went home ?

Liff. I can give you very good Reasons for my Stay, Si ——Yes Sir, she went home.

Fred O ! Your Master knows that, for he has been there himself, *Liffardo*

Liff. Sir, may I beg the Favour of your Ear ?

Fel. What have you to say ? [*Whispers, and Felix*
seems uneasy]

Fred Ha, *Felix* changes Colour at *Liffardo's* New*. What can it be ?

Fel. A *Scots* Footman, that belongs to Colonel *Britton,* an Acquaintance of *Frederick's,* say you ? the Devil ! if she be false, by Heaven I'll trace he Prithy, *Frederick,* do you know one Colonel *Britton,* a Scotchman ?

Fred. Yes ; why do you ask me ?

Fel Nay, no great Matter, but my Man tells me that he has had some little Differences with a Servant of his, that's all.

Fred. He is a good harmless innocent Fellow, I am sorry for it ; the Colonel lodges in my House, I knew him formerly in *England,* and met him here by Accident last Night, and gave him an Invitation home ; he is a Gentleman of a good Eftate, befides his Commiffion ; of excellent Principles, and ftrict Honour, I affure you.

Fel. Is he a Man of Intrigue ?

Fred Like other Men, I fuppofe ; here he comes ——

[*Enter* Colonel.

Colonel, I began to think I had loft you

Col ——And not without fome Reafon, if you knew all.

Fel There's no Danger of a fine Gentleman's being loft in this Town, Sir

Col That Compliment don't belong to me, Sir But I affure you I have been very near being run away with.

Fred Who attempted it ?

Col Faith, I know her not—— Only that fhe is a charming Woman, I mean as much as I faw of her

Fel My Heart fwells with Apprehenfion —— fome accidental Rencounter ——

Fred A Tavern, I fuppofe, adjufted the Matter ——

Col A Tavern ! No, no, Sir, fhe is above that Rank, I affure you, this Nymph fleeps in a Velvet bed, and Lodgings every way agreeable

Fel. Ha, a Velvet Bed !—I thought you faid but now Sir, you knew her not.

Col. No more I don't, Sir.

Fel How came you then fo well acquainted with her Bed ?

Fred Ay ay, come, come, unfold.

Col Why then you muft know, Gentlemen, that I was convey'd to her Lodgings, by one of Cupid's Emiffaries, call'd a Chambermaid, in a Chair thro' fifty blind Alleys, who by the Help of a Key let me into a Garden.

Fel. 'Sdeath, a Garden, this muft be *Ifclante*'s Garden. [*Afide.*

Col From thence conducted me into a fpacious Room, then dropt me a Courtefy, told me her Lady would wait on me prefently, fo without unveiling, modeftly withdrew.

Fel Damn her Modefty, this was *Flora* [*Afide.*

Fred Well, how then, Colonel ?

Col. Then, Sir, immediately from another Door iffued forth a Lady, arm'd at both Eyes, from whence fuch Showers of Darts fell round me, that had I not been cover'd with the Shield of another Beauty, I had

C 4 infallibly

in'vitably fall'n a Martyr to her Charms; for you must know, I just saw her Eyes——Eyes did I say? no, no, hold. I saw but one Eye, though I suppose it had a Fellow, equally as killing

Fel But how came you to see her Bed, Sir? 'Sdeath, this Expectation gives a thousand Racks.   [*Aside.*

Col Why, upon her Maid's giving Notice her Father was coming, she thrust me into the Bed-Chamber.

Fel Upon her Father's coming?

Col. Ay, so she said; but putting my Ear to the Key-Hole of the Door, I found it was another Lover

Fel Confound the Jilt! 'Twas she without Dispute.
                                                        [*Aside.*

Fred Ah poor Colonel, ha, ha, ha

Col I discover'd they had had a Quarrel, but whether they were reconcil'd or not, I can't tell; for the second Alarm brought the Father in good earnest, and had like to have made the Gentleman and I acquainted, but she found some other Stratagem to convey him out.

Fel Contagion seize her, and make her Body ugly as her Soul. There is nothing left to doubt of now.—— 'Tis plain 'twas she——Sure he knows me, and takes this Method to insult me; 'Sdeath I cannot bear it [*Aside.*

Fred So when she had dispatch'd her old Lover, she paid you a Visit in her Bed-chamber; ha, Colonel?

Col No, Pox take the impertinent Puppy, he spoil'd my Diversion, I saw her no more

Fel. Very fine! give me Patience, Heaven, or I shall burst with Rage   [*Aside.*

Fred. That was hard.

Col Nay, what was worse, the Nymph that introduced me conveyed me out again over the Top of a high Wall, where I ran the danger of having my Neck broke, for the Father it seems had locked the Door by which I enter'd.

Fel That Way I miss'd him ·—— Damn her Invention (*Aside*) Pray, Colonel, was this the same Lady you met upon the *Terreiro de passa* this Morning?

Col Faith, I can't tell, Sir, I had a Design to know who that Lady was, but my Dog of a Footman, whom I had order'd to watch her home, fell fast asleep —— I
                                                              gave

gave him a good Beating for his Neglect, and I have never seen the Rascal since.

Fred Here he comes.

Enter Gibby.

Col. Where have you been, Sirrah ?

Gib. Troth Ife been seeking vee an like ver Honour these twa Hoors an meer   I bring yee glad Teedings, Sir

Col What, have you found the Lady ?

Gib Geud Faite, ha I Sir—an she's call'd *Donna Vo-lante*, and her Parent *Don Pedro de Mendoza* en gin yee will gan wa mi, an't lik yer Honour, Ife make yee ken the Huse right weel.

Fel O Torture ! Torture !   [*Aside*

Col. Ha ! *Violante !* That's the Lady's Name of the House where my Incognita is, sure it could not be her, at least it was not the same House, I'm confident.

[*Aside*

Fred. Violante ? 'Tis false ; I would not have you credit him, Colonel

Gib. The Deel burst my Bladder, Sir, gin I lee.

Fel. Sirrah, I say you do lye, and I'll make you eat it, you Dog, *(kicks him)* and if your Master will justify you————

Col Not I, faith, Sir,—I answer for no body's Lyes but my own , if you please, kick him again.

Gib. But gin he dus, Ife ne take it, Sir, gin he was a thousand *Spaniards.*   [*walks about in a passion.*

Col I ow'd you a Beating, Sirrah, and I'm oblig'd to this Gentleman for taking the Trouble off my Hands ; therefore say no more, d'ye hear, Sir ? [*Aside to* Gibby.

Gib Troth de I, Sir, and feel tee

Fred This must be a Mistake, Colonel, for I know *Violante* perfectly well, and I am certain she would not meet you upon the *Terreiro de passa*

Col. Don't be too positive, *Frederic*, now I have some Reasons to believe it was that very Lady

Fel You'd very much oblige me, Sir, if you'd let me know these Reasons.

Col. Sir ?

Fel Sir, I say I have a Right to enquire into these Reasons you speak of.

C 5

Col.

Col Ha, ha, re liv, Sir? I cannot conceive how you or any Man can have a Right to enquire into my Thoughts

Fel Sir, I have a Right to every Thing that relates to *Violante* — And he that traduces her Fame, and refuses to give his Reasons for't, is a Villain   [*Draws.*

Col What the Devil have I been doing? now Blisters on my Tongue, by Dozens   [*Aside*

Fred Prithee, *Felix*, don't quarrel, till you know for what, this is all a Mistake I'm positive

Col Look ye, Sir, that I dare draw my Sword, I think will admit of no Dispute ———— But tho' fighting's my Trade, I'm not in love with it, and think it more honourable to decline this Business, than pursue it   This may be a Mistake, however I'll give you my Honour never to have any Affair directly, or indirectly with *Violante*, provided she is your *Violante*, but if there should happen to be another of her Name, I hope you would not engross all the *Violantes* in the Kingdom.

Fel Your Vanity has given me sufficient Reasons to believe I'm not mistaken; I'll not be impos'd upon, Sir,

Col Nor I bully'd, Sir

Fel Bully'd! 'Sdeath, such another Word, and I'll nail thee to the Wall

Col Are you sure of that *Spaniard?*   [*Draws.*

Gib (*Draws*) Say ne meer, Mon, aw my Sol here's Twa to Twa, dena fear, Sir, *Gibby* stonds by ye for the Honour of *Scotland*   [*Vapours about.*

Fred By St. *Anthony* you shan't fight (*Interposes*) on bare Suspicion, be certain of the Injury, and then——

Fel That I will this Moment, and then, Sir——I hope you are to be found———

Col Where'er you please, Sir   [*Exit Felix.*

Gib 'bleed, Sir, there neer was a *Scotsman* yet that sham'd to show his Face   [*Strutting about.*

Fred So, Quarrels spring up like Mushrooms, in a Minute   *Violante* and he were but just reconcil'd, and you have furnish'd him with fresh Matter for falling out again, and I am certain, Colonel, *Gibby* is in the Wrong.

Gib.

Gib Gin I be, Sr, the Man that tald me leed, and gin he dud, the Deel be my Landlard, Hell my Winter quarters, and a Rope my Winding sheet, gin I dee not lik him as larg as I can ho'd a Stick in my Hond, row see yee

Col I am sorry for what I have said, for the Lady's Ske, but who could divine that she was his Mistress? Prithee, who is this warm Spark?

Fred He is the Son of one of our Giardees, nam'd *Don Lopez de Pimentell*, a very honest Gentleman, but something passionate in what relates to his Love —— He is an only Son, which may perhaps be one Reason for indulging his Passion

Col When Parents have but one Child, they either make a Madman or a Fool of him

Fred He is not the only Child, he has a Sister, but I think, thro' the Severity of his Father, who would have married her against her Inclination, she has made her Escape, and notwithstanding he has offered five hundred Pounds, he can get no Tidings of her.

Col Ha! how long has she been missing?

Fred Nay, but since last Night, it seems

Col Last Night! The very Time! How went she?

Fred No body can tell, they conjecture thro' the Window

Col I'm transported! This must be the Lady I caught. What sort of a Woman is she?

Fred Middle siz'd, a lovely brown, a fine pouting Lip, Eyes that roll and languish, and seem to speak the exquisite Pleasure her Arms could give!

Col Oh! I'm fir'd with this Description—— 'Tis the very she——What's her Name?

Fred *Isabella*————You are transported, Colonel.

Col I have a natural Tendency in me to the Flesh, thou know'st, and who can hear of Charms so exquisite and yet remain unmov'd? Oh, how I long for the appointed Hour! I'll to the *Terriro de passa*, and wait my Happiness, if she fails to meet me, I'll once more attempt to find her at *Violante's* in spite of her Brother's Jealousy. [*Aside*] Dear *Frederick*, I beg your Pardon, but I had forgot, I was to meet a Gentleman upon Bu-

siness

finefs at Five, I'll endeavour to difpatch him, and wait on you again as foon as poffible.————

Fred Your humble Servant. Colonel.   [*Exit.*

Col. Gibby, I have no Bufinefs with you at prefent.
                                        [*Exit* Colonel.

Gib That's weel————naw will I gang and feek this Loon, and gar him gang with me to *Don Pedro*'s Hufe.————Gin he'll no gang of himfel, Iſe gar him gang by the Lug, Sir, Godfwarbit, *Gibby* hates a Lear.   [*Exit.*

Scene changes to VIOLANTE'*s Lodging*

Enter Violante *and* Ifabella

Ifab The Hour draws on, *Violante*, and now my Heart begins to fail me, but I refolve to venture for all that

Vio What, does your Courage fink, *Ifabella* ?

Ifab Only the Force of Refolution a little retreated, but I'll rally it again for all that.

Enter Flora

Flo Don *Felix* is coming up, Madam.

Ifa! My Brother! Which way fhall I get out ————Difpatch him as foon as you can, dear *Violante*
                                [*Exit into the Clofet.*

Vio I will. (*Enter* Felix *in a furly pofture.*) *Felix*, what brings you home fo foon, did I not fay to-morrow ?

Fel My Paffion choaks me, I cannot fpeak; Oh ! I fhall burit! [*Afide.*]   [*Throws himfelf into a Chair.*

Vio Blefs me, are you not well, my *Felix* ?

Fel Yes,——No,—— I don't know what I am.

Vio Hey Day ! What's the Matter now ? Another jealous Whim !

Fel With what an Air fhe carries it !——— I fweat at her Impudence   [*Afide.*

Vio If I were in your Place, *Felix*, I'd chufe to ftay at home, when thefe Fits of Spleen are upon me, and not trouble fuch Perfons as are not obliged to bear with them   (*Here he affects to be carelefs of her.*

Fel I am very fenfible, Madam, of what you mean : I difturb you, no doubt, but were I in a better Humour I fhould not incommode you lefs. I am but too well convinc'd you could eafily difpenfe with my Vifit.

Vio. When you behave yourfelf as you ought to do,
                                                        no

no Company fo welcome—But when you referve me for your ill Nature, I wave your Merit, and confider what's due to myfelf—And I muft be fo free to tell you, *Felix*, that thefe Humours of yours will abate, if not abfolutely deftroy the very Principles of Love.

Fel (Rifing) And I muft be fo free to tell you, Madam, that fince you have made fuch ill Returns to the Refpect that I have paid you, all you do fhall be indifferent to me for the future, and you fhall find me abandon your Empire with fo little Difficulty, that I'll convince the World your Chains are not fo hard to break as your Vanity would tempt you to believe——I cannot brook the Provocation you give.

Vio. This is not to be borne—Infolent! You abandon! You! Whom I have fo often forbad ever to fee me more! Have you not fall'n at my Feet! Implor'd my Favour and Forgivenefs?—Did not you trembling wait, and wifh, and figh, and fwear yourfelf into my Heart? Ungrateful Man! If my Chains are fo eafily broke, as you pretend, then you are the filliest Coxcomb living you did not break 'em long ago, and I muft think him capable of brooking any thing on whom fuch Ufage could make no Impreffion.

Hab (Peeping) A Duce take your Quarrels, fhe'll never think on me

Fe. I always believed, Madam, my Weaknefs was the greateft Addition to your Power; you wou'd be lefs imperious, had my Inclination been lefs forward to oblige you ——You have indeed forbad me your Sight, but your Vanity even then affured you I would return, and I was Fool enough to feed your Pride—Your Eyes, with all their boafted Charms, have acquired the greateft Glory in conquering me —And the brighteft Paffion of your Life is, wounding this Heart with fuch Arms as pierce but few Perfons of my Rank

[*Walks about in a great Pet.*

Vio. Matchlefs Arrogance! True, Sir, I fhould have kept Meafures better with you, if the Conqueft had been worth preferving; but we eafily hazard what gives us no Pain to lofe ——As for my Eyes, you are miftaken if you think they have vanquifhed none but
you;

you, there are Men above your boasted Rank who have confess'd their Power, when their Misfortune in pleasing you made them obtain such a disgraceful Victory.

Fel. Yes, Madam, I am no Stranger to your Victories

Vio. And what you call the brightest Passage of my Life, is not the least glorious Part of yours

Fel. Ha, ha, don't put yourself into a Passion, Madam, for I assure you, after this Day, I shall give you no Trouble —You may meet your Sparks on the *Terriero de passa* at four in the Morning, without the least Regard to mine—For when I quit your Chamber, the World shan't bring me back.

Vio. I am so well pleas'd with your Resolution, I don't care how soon you take your Leave.—But what you mean by the *Terriero de passa* at four in the Morning, I can't guess

Fel. No, no, no, not you——You was not upon the *Terriero de passa* at Four this Morning.

Vio. No, I was not; but if I was, I hope I may walk where I please, and at what Hour I please, without asking your leave.

Fel. Oh, doubtless, Madam! And you might meet Colonel *Britton* there, and afterwards send your Emissary to fetch him to your House ———And upon your Father's coming in, thrust him into your Bed-chamber —without asking my leave 'Tis no Business of mine if you are expos'd among all the Footmen in Town —Nay, if they Ballad you, and cry you about at a Halfpenny a piece——They may without my Leave.

Vio. Audacious! Don't provoke me——don't, my Reputation is not to be sported with, *(going up to him)* at this Rate —No, Sir, it is not, *(bursts into tears)* Inhuman *Felix!*——Oh, *Isabella,* what a Train of Ills hast thou brought on me! [*Aside.*

Fel. Ha! I cannot bear to see her weep —A Woman's Tears are far more fatal than our Swords. [*Aside.* Oh, *Violante*——'Sdeath! what a Dog am I? Now have I no Power to stir —Dost not thou know such a Person as Colonel *Britton?* Prithee tell me, didst not thou meet him at Four this Morning upon the *Terriero de passa?*   *Vio.*

Vio. Were it not to clear my Fame, I would not anfwer thee, thou black Ingrate!——— But I cannot bear to be reproached with what I even blufh to think of, much lefs to act, by Heaven, I have not feen the *Terrero de paffa* this Day

Fel. Did not a *Scots* Footman attack you in the Street neither, *Violante?*

Vio. Yes, but he miftook me for another, or he was drunk, I know not which

Fel. And do not you know this *Scots* Colonel?

Vio. Pray afk me no more Queftions, this Night fhall clear my Reputation, and leave you without Excufe for your bafe Sufpicions; more than this I fhall not fatisfy you, therefore pray Leave me.

Fel. Didft thou ever love me, *Violante?*

Vio. I'll anfwer nothing.———You was in hafte to be gone juft now, I fhould be very well pleas'd to be alone, Sir. *(She fits down and turns afide.*

Fel. I fhall not long interrupt your Contemplation. ——Stubborn to the laft. *[Afide.*

Vio. Did ever Woman involve herfelf as I have done?

Fel. Now would I give one of my Eyes to be Friends with her, for fomething whifpers to my Soul fhe is not guilty. ———*(He paufes, then pulls a Chair, and fits by her at a little Diftance, looking at her fome time without fpeaking.——Then draws a little nearer to her)* Give me your Hand at Parting however, *Violante,* won't you, *(Here he lays his open upon her Knee feveral times.)* won't you———won't you——— won't you?

Vio. *(Half regarding him)* Won't I do what?

Fel. You know what I would have, *Violante.* Oh, my Heart!

Vio. *(Smiling)* I thought my Chairs were eafi'y broke *(Lays her Hand into his)*

Fel. *(Draws his Chair clofe to her, and kiffes her Hand in a Rapture)* Too well thou knoweft thy Strength———Oh my charming Angel, my Heart is all thy own. Forgive my hafty Paffion, 'tis the Tranfport of a Love fincere!

Don Pedro *within*

Pedro Bid *Sancho* get a new Wheel to my Chariot prefently.

Vio.

Vio. Blefs me ! my Father return'd ! what fhall we do now, *Felix* ! We are ruin'd, paft Redemption.

Fel No, no, no, my Love; I can leap from thy Clofet Window. (*Runs to the Door where* Ifabella *is, who claps too the Door, and bolts it within fide.*

Ifab (*Peeping*) Say you fo But I fhall prevent you.

Fel Confufion ! Some body bolts the Door within fide , I'll fee who you have conceal'd here, if I die for't; Oh *Violante* ! haft thou again facrific'd me to my Rival   (*Draws.*

Vio By Heaven thou haft no Rival in my Heart, let that fuffice—Nay, fure, you will not let my Father find you here———Diftraction !

Fel. Indeed but I fhall—except you command this Door to be open'd, and that way conceal me from his Sight.   [*He ftruggles with her to come at the Door.*

Vio. Hear me, *Felix*———Though I were fure the refufing what you afk would feparate us for ever, by all that's powerful you fhall not enter here • Either you do love me, or you do not , convince me by your Obedience

Fel That's not the Matter in debate—I will know who is in this Clofet, let the Confequence be what it will. Nay, nav, nay, you ftrive in vain, I will go in

Vio. You fhall not go in———

Enter Don Pedro.

Ped Hey day ! What's here to do ! I will go in, and, You fhan't go in———and, I will go in——— Why, who are you, Sir ?

Fel 'Sdeath ! What fhall I fay now ?

Ped. Don Felix, pray what's your Bufinefs in my Houfe ? Ha, Sir.

Vio. On Sir, what Miracle return'd you home fo foon ? Some Angel 'twas that brought my Father back to fuccour the Diftrefs'd ———This Ruffian he, I cannot call him Gentleman———has committed fuch an uncommon Rudenefs, as the moft profligate Wretch would be afham'd to own———

Fel. Ha, what the Devil does fhe mean !   (*Afid.*
j 10.

Vio. As I was at my Devotion in my Closet, I heard a loud Knocking at the Door, mix'd with a Woman's Voice, which seem'd to imply she was in Danger——

Fel. I am confounded! (*Aside.*

Vio. I flew to the Door with the utmost Speed, where a Lady veil'd rush'd in upon me, who falling on her Knees begged my Protection, from a Gentleman, who, she said, pursued her. I took Compassion on her Tears, and lock'd her into this Closet; but in the Surprize, having left open the Door, this very Person whom you see, with his Sword drawn, ran in, protesting, if I refus'd to give her up to his Revenge, he'd force the Door.

Fel. What in the Name of Goodness does she mean to do! Hang me! (*Aside.*

Vio. I strove with him till I was out of Breath, and had you not come as you did, he must have enter'd— but he's in drink, I suppose, or he could not have been guilty of such an Indecorum. [*Leering at* Felix.

Ped. I'm amaz'd!

Fel. The Devil never fail'd a Woman at a Pinch: what a Tale has she form'd in a Minute——In drink, quotha; a good hint; I'll lay hold on't to bring my-self off (*Aside.*

Ped. Fie, *Don Felix!* No sooner rid of one Broil, but you are commencing another—to assault a Lady with a naked Sword, derogates much from the Character of a Gentleman, I assure you.

Fel. (*Counterfeits Drunkenness*) Who, I assault a Lady ——upon Honour the Lady assaulted me, Sir; and would have seiz'd this Body Politick upon the King's Highway——let her come out, and deny it if she can ——pray, Sir, command the Door to be open'd, and let her prove me a Liar if she knows how——I have been drinking right *French* Claret, Sir, but I love my own Country for all that.

Ped. Ay, ay, who doubts it, Sir?—Open the Door, *Violante,* and let the Lady come out—Come, I warrant thee he shan't hurt her.

Fel. Ay, now which way will she come off.

Vio. (*Unlocks the Door*) Come forth, Madam, none shall dare to touch your Veil——I'll convey you out
with

with Safety, or lose my Life——I hope she understands
me.　　　　　　　　　　　　　　　　　　　　(*Aside.*

Enter Isabella *veil'd and crosses the Stage*

Isab. Excellent Girl!　　　　　　　　　　　(*Exit*

Fel. The Devil! a Woman! I'll see if she be really
so.　　　　　　　　　　　　　(*Offers to follow her*

Ped. (*Draws*) Not a Step, Sir, till the Lady be past
your Recovery.——I never suffer the Laws of Hospita-
lity to be violated in my House, Sir —— I'll keep *Don
Felix* here till you see her safe out, *Isclante.*

Vio. Get clear of my Father, and follow me to the
Terriero de passa, where all Mistakes shall be rectified.
(*Aside to* Felix)　　　　　　　　　　[*Exit* Violante

Ped. Come, Sir, you and I will take a Pipe and a
Bottle together.

Fel. Damn your Pipe, Sir, I won't smoak——I hate
Tobacco——Nor I, I, I, I won't drink, Si —————No
nor I won't stay neither, and how will you help yourself?

Ped. As to smoaking or drinking, you have your
Liberty, but you shall stay, Sir.　　(*Gets between him
and the Door,* Felix *strikes up his Heels and Exit.*

Fel. Shall I so, Sir?——But I tell you, old Gentleman, I am in haste to be married——And so God be
with you.

Ped. Go to the Devil—In haste to be married, quotha,
thou art in a fine Condition to be married truly!

Enter a Servant.

Ser. Here's *Don Lopez de Pimentell* to wait on you,
Senior

Ped. What the Devil does he want? Bring him up,
he's in Pursuit of his Son I suppose

Enter Don Lopez

Lop. I am glad to find you at home, *Don Pedro,* I
was told that you was seen upon the Road to——this
Afternoon

Ped. That might be, my Lord, but I had the Misfortune to break the Wheel of my Chariot, which oblig'd
me to return——What is your Pleasure with me, my
Lord?

Lop. I am inform'd that my Daughter's in your
House, *Don Pedro.*

　　　　　　　　　　　　　　　　　　　　Ped.

Ped That's more than I know, my Lord, but here was your Son juft now as drunk as an Emperor.

Ped My Con drunk! I never faw him in drink in my Life; wheie is he, pray, Sir?

Ped Gone to be married.

Lop. Married! To whom? I don't know that he courted any Body.

Ped. Nay, I know nothing of that —— Within there! [*Enter Servant*] bid my Daughter come hither, fhe'l tell you another Story, my Lord

Ser She's gone out in a Chair, Sir.

Ped. Out in a Chair! What do you mean, Sir?

Ser. As I fay, Sir, and *Donna Ifabella* went in another juft before her

Ser And *Don Felix* followed in another, I overheard them all bid the Chairs go to the *Terriero de prefa*.

Ped Ha! What Bufinefs has my Daughter there? I am confounded and know not what to think.————
Within there. [*Exit.*

Lop My Heart mifgives me plaguily ———Call me an *Alguazile*, I'll purfue them ftrait.

SCENE *changes to the Street before* Don Pedro's *Houfe.*

Enter Liflardo

Lif I wifh I cou'd fee *Flora* ——— Methinks I have an hankering Kindnefs after the Slut——— We muft be reconcil'd

Enter Gibby.

Gib Aw my Sol, Sir, but I'e blithe to find yee here now.

Lif Ha! Brother! Give me thy Hand, Boy

Gib No fe faft, fe ye me—Brether, me ne Brethers, I fcorn a Lyar as muckle as a Thiefe, fe ye now, and yee muft gang intul this Houfe with me, and juftifie to *Donna Violante's* Face, that fhe was the Lady that gang'd in here this Morn, fe yee me, or the Deel ha my Sol, Sir, but ye and I fhall be twa Folks

Lif Juftify it to *Donna Violante's* Face, quotha, for what? Sure you don't know what you fay

Gib.

Gib. Troth de I, Sir, as weel as yee de; therefore come along, and make no meer Words about it.

[*Knocks hastily at the Door.*

Lif. Why, what the Devil do you mean? Don't you confider you are in *Portugal?* Is the Fellow mad?

Gib. Fallow! Ife none of yer Fallow, Sir, and gin this be e'ere Ifell, and gar ye de me Justice, [*Lif. going*] nay the Deel a Feet ye gang. [*Lays hold of him, and knocks again.*

Enter Don Pedro

Ped. How now! what makes you knock so loud?

Gib. Gin this be *Don Pedro's* House, Sir, I wou'd speak with *Donna Violante*, his Daughter

Lif. Ha! *Don Pedro* himself, I wish I were fairly off   [*Afide.*

Ped. Ha! What is't you want with my Daughter, pray?

Gib. An she be your Daughter, and't like your Honour, command her to come forth, and answer for herself now, and either justify or difprove what this Shield told me this Morn.

Lif. So, here will be a fine Piece of Work.   [*Afide.*

Ped. Why, what did he tell you, ha?

Gib. By my Sol, Sir, Ife tell you aw the Truth; my Master got a pretty Lady upon one how de ye call't——*Paffa*——here at Five this Morn, and he gar me watch her heam——And in Troth I lodg'd her here, and meeting this ill favour'd Thiefe, fe ye me, I fpiered wha she was——An he told me her Name was *Donna Violante, Don Pedro de Mendofa's* Daughter

Ped. Ha! My Daughter with a Man abroad at Five in the Morning. Death, Hell, and Furies, by St. *Anthony* I'm undone   [*Stamps.*

Gib. Wounds, Sir, ye put yer Saint intul bony Company.

Ped. Who is your Master, you Dog you? Adfheart I shall be trick'd of my Daughter, and my Money too, that's worst of all.

Gib. Ye Dog you! 'Sblead, Sir, don't call Names—— I won't tell you wha my Master is, fe ye me now.

Ped.

Ped And who are you, Rafcal, that knows my Daughter fo well? Ha! *(Holds up his Cane.*

Liff. What fhall I fay to make him give this *Scots* Dog a good beating? *(Afide)* I know your Daughter, *Senior?* Not I, I never faw your Daughter in all my Life.

Gib. *(Knocks him down with his Fift)* Deel ha my Sol, Sar, gin ye get no your Carich for that Lye now

Ped. What, hoa! Where are all my Servants? *(Enter Servants on one Side,* Colonel, Felix, Ifabella, *and* Violante *on the other Side)* Raife the Houfe in purfuit of my Daughter

Serv Here fhe comes, *Senior.*

Col. Hey Day! What's here to do?

Gib This is the Loon like 'Tik, an lik yer Honour, that fent me heam with a Lye this Morn

Col. Come, come, 'tis all well, *Gibby,* let him rife.

Ped I am Thunder-ftruck—and have no Power to fpeak one Word.

Fel This is a Day of Jubilee, *Liffardo,* no quarreling with him this Day.

Liff. A Pox take his Fifts.——Egad thefe *Britons* are but a Word and a Blow.

Enter Don Lopez

Lop. So, have I found you, Daughter? Then you have not hang'd yourfelf yet, I fee.

Col. But fhe is married, my Lord.

Lop Married! Zounds, to whom?

Col. Even to your humble Servant, my Lord. If you pleafe to give us your Bleffing. *(Kneels.*

Lop. Why, hark ye, Miftrefs, are you really married?

Ifab. Really fo, my Lord.

Lop. And who are you, Sir?

Col An honeft *North Britain* by Birth, and a Colonel by Commiffion, my Lord

Lop. An Heretic! The Devil! *(Holding up his Hands.*

Ped She has play'd you a flippery Trick indeed, my Lord —Well, my Girl, thou haft been to fee thy Friend married.——Next Week thou fhalt have a better Hufband, my Dear. [*To* Violante.]

Fel Next Week is a little too foon, Sir; I hope to live longer than that.

2

Ped.

Ped What do you mean, Sir? you have not made a Rib of my Daughter too, have you?

Vio. Indeed but he has, Sir, I know not how, but he took me in an unguarded Minute,—when my Thoughts were not over-strong for a Nunnery, Father

Lop Your Daughter has play'd you a flippery Trick too, *Senior*.

Ped But your Son shall never be the better for't, my Lord; her twenty thousand Pounds was left on certain Conditions, and I'll not part with a Shilling

Lop But we have a certain Thing call'd Law, shall make you do Justice, Sir

Ped. Well, we'll try that,—my Lord, much good may it do you with your Daughter-in-Law 　　*(Exit*

Lop I wish you much Joy of your Rib 　　*(Exit*

Enter Frederick

Fel. Frederick, welcome!——I sent for thee to be Witness of my good Fortune, and make one in a Country Dance.

Fred. Your Messenger has told me all, and I sincerely share in all your Happiness

Col. To the Right about, *Frederick*; wish thy Friend Joy.

Fred I do with all my Soul,—and, Madam, I congratulate your Deliverance—Your Suspicions are clear'd now, I hope, *Felix*.

Fel They are, and I heartily ask the Colonel Pardon, and wish him happy with my Sister, for Love has taught me to know, that every Man's Happiness consists in chusing for himself.

Liss After that Rule I fix here. 　　[*To* Flora.

Flo That's your Mistake, I prefer my Lady's Service, and turn you over to her that pleaded Right and Title to you To-day.

Liss. Chuse, proud Fool; I shant ask you twice

Gib. What say ye now, Lass, will ye ge yer Maidenhead to poor *Gibby*?——What say you, will ye dance the Reel of *Bogie* with me?

Ims. That I may not leave my Lady—I take you at your Word,—And tho' our Wooing has been short, I'll by her Example love you dearly. 　　[*Musick plays.*

I

Fel.

Fel Hark ! I hear the Mufick ; fomebody has done us the Favour to fend them, call them in.

A Country Dance.

Gib Wounds, this is bony Mufick—— How caw ye that Thing that ye pinch by the Craig, and tickle the Weam, ond make it cry, *Grum, Grum?*

Fred Oh ! that's a Guitar, *Gibby*

Fel. Now, my *Violante*, I fhall proclaim thy Virtues to the World.

> *No more let us thy Sex's Conduct blame,*
> *Since thou'rt a Proof to their eternal Fame,*
> *That* Man *has no Advantage but the Name.* }

EPILOGUE.

Written by Mr. PHILIPS.

CUstom, with all our Modern Laws combin'd,
Has given such Power despotic to Mankind,
That we have only so much Virtue now,
As they are pleas'd in favour to allow
Thus like Mechanic Work we're us'd with Scorns,
And wound up only for a present Turn,
Some are for having our whole Sex enslav'd,
Affirming we've no Souls *and can't be sav'd.
But were the Women all of my Opinion,
We'd soon shake off this false usurp'd Dominion
We'd make the Tyrants own, that we cou'd prove,
As fit for other Business as for Love
Lord! What Prerogative might we obtain,
Could we from Yielding, a few Months refrain!
How fond'y wou'd our dang'ling Lovers doat?
What Homage wou'd be paid to Petticoat?
'Twou'd be a Jest to see the Change of Fate,
How might we all of Politicks debate;
Promise and swear what we ne'er meant to do,
And what's still harder, Keep our Secrets too.
Ay, Marry! Keep a Secret, says a Beau,
And sneers at some ill-natur'd Wit below;
But faith, if we show'd tell but half we know,
There's many a spruce young Fellow in this Place,
Wou'd never more presume to show his Face,
Women are not so weak, whate'er Men prate;
How many tip-top Beaus have had the Fate,
T' enjoy from Mamma's Secrets their Estate
Who, if her early Folly had made known,
Had rid behind the Coach that's now their own.
But here the Wond'rous Secret you discover;
A Lady ventures for a Friend,————A Lover.
Prodigious! for my Part I frankly own,
I'ad spoil'd the Wonder, and the Woman shown.

*Alluding to an ironical Pamphlet tending to prove that
Women had no Souls.

FINIS.

CPSIA information can be obtained
at www.ICGtesting.com
Printed in the USA
LVHW101334050819
626550LV00012B/243/P